I0762910

"In the academy, the parish, and the public square, one of the most persistent and pressing questions revolves around the trustworthiness of the Christian Gospels. Gathercole responds to that concern with *The Genuine Jesus and the Counterfeit Christs*, an inviting conversation built upon complex scholarship. Readers are not only assured *that* the four canonical Gospels are trustworthy but are given the tools to understand *why*, because they come to understand *who* the evangelists proclaim Jesus to be. I cannot wait to recommend this rich and accessible guide to students, parishioners, and neighbors alike."

—**Amy Peeler,** Wheaton College

"Simon Gathercole's *The Genuine Jesus and the Counterfeit Christs* gets to the heart of why the four Gospels are genuine: they embody the message of Christ and the apostles, a message that fulfills Old Testament expectations. The apocryphal gospels, though, don't reflect this message. This learned yet accessible volume deserves wide readership and belongs on the shelves of lay people, students, pastors, and teachers. Highly recommended!"

—**Benjamin L. Gladd**
The Carson Center for Theological Renewal

"In *The Genuine Jesus and the Counterfeit Christs,* Simon Gathercole debunks popular arguments about how various ancient sources rival the validity of the four New Testament Gospels. Gathercole concisely presents evidence that the four Gospels are early in composition, accurate in telling the story of Jesus, and united on the core truths about his life, teaching, and saving death and resurrection. Matthew, Mark, Luke, and John deserve to be in a category of their own, and they belong in the New Testament as a fourfold witness to Jesus Christ. This is an excellent book to assign to students or share with fellow church members."

—**Nijay K. Gupta,** Northern Seminary

The Genuine Jesus and the Counterfeit Christs

New Testament and Apocryphal Gospels

Simon Gathercole

William B. Eerdmans Publishing Company
Grand Rapids, Michigan

Wm. B. Eerdmans Publishing Co.
2006 44th Street SE, Grand Rapids, MI 49508
www.eerdmans.com

Published 2025
Printed in the United States of America

31 30 29 28 27 26 25 1 2 3 4 5 6 7

ISBN 978-0-8028-8445-9

Library of Congress Cataloging-in-Publication Data

A catalog record for this book is available from the Library of Congress.

Contents

Introduction

The four Gospels that made it into the
official canon were chosen, more or less
arbitrarily, out of a larger sample of at least
a dozen including the Gospels of Thomas,
Peter, Nicodemus, Philip, Bartholomew and
Mary Magdalen.[1]

These words from Richard Dawkins's book *The God Delusion* sum up a common view of the Gospels outside the New Testament.[2] What should we make of these Gospels of Thomas, Peter, and Mary Magdalene that he's talking about? Do they really exist, or are they just part of an atheist conspiracy theory that imagines that there must have been more than just Matthew, Mark, Luke, and John?

The truth in Dawkins's statement is that there really was a large sample of Gospels, usually called "apocryphal" or "noncanonical" Gospels, other than just the four in the New Testament. We know this because ancient Christian authors refer to them. We also have actual manuscripts of many of them, which show that they really are ancient texts. So they differ from two other Gospels that have sometimes attracted publicity. One of these is the *Gospel of Barnabas*, an Islamic book that argues that Jesus was preparing the way for Muhammad. This is not a genuinely ancient work: it comes from late on in the Middle Ages.[3] The other is the *Gospel of Jesus' Wife*, which was allegedly "discovered" in 2012. After a buzz of media attention, detective work on the seller of the manuscript and scholarly analysis of the text both showed that the manuscript was a forgery. Scholars demonstrated that the text was copied from a website containing the *Gospel of Thomas*, because the *Gospel of Jesus' Wife* fragment reproduced one of the Coptic language mistakes on this website. And investigative journalist Ariel Sabar identified the forger as a former Egyptology student from Germany who, via curating a museum, working in a car-parts business, and a stint in online pornography, became a dealer in forged manuscripts and eventually admitted the manuscript was a modern fake.[4] But the Gospels that Dawkins mentions, as well as those discussed in this book here, do really come from the Roman Empire in the early centuries of the Christian era (though scholars don't usually consider them to be as old as the Gospels in the New Testament). In fact, Dawkins's reference to "a dozen" is a bit of an underestimate. One scholar in 2005 wrote an article entitled "Forty Other Gospels."[5] And there have been more manuscripts of other Gospel texts discovered even since then. This book is not going to cover all of these Gospels. It's going to focus in on Matthew, Mark, Luke, and John, as well as seven of the best-preserved and best-known apocryphal Gospels.

Where Dawkins and others go wrong is in thinking that there's something just "arbitrary" about the four New Testament Gospels belonging together, and nothing really distinctive about Matthew, Mark, Luke, and John. The main point of this book is to show otherwise, and to make this point by arguing for two propositions:

PROPOSITION 1

The four New Testament Gospels share key elements of theological content that mark them out from most of the noncanonical Gospels.

PROPOSITION 2

The reason why the four New Testament Gospels are theologically similar to one another is that they—unlike most others— follow the existing gospel message of the apostles.

The first point, then, is just about what the Gospels say—that the four New Testament works contain presentations of Jesus that in crucial ways are similar to each other, but that the apocryphal Gospels discussed here are different. The second argument is that this is not a historical accident: the reason the portraits of Jesus in the four Gospels are similar is that they all emerge out of the same form of Christianity, and follow what the apostles preached. But the apocryphal Gospels surveyed here come out of different religious stables.

We can begin by learning what these early apocryphal Gospels are about.

CHAPTER ONE

What Are the Other Gospels?

This first chapter will introduce the most important of the apocryphal Gospels—the *Gospel of Peter,* the *Gospel of Thomas,* Marcion's Gospel, the *Gospel of Truth,* the *Gospel of Philip,* the Coptic *Gospel of the Egyptians,* and the *Gospel of Judas.* I will also mention the *Gospel of Mary*. Alongside these, this book will of course cover the New Testament Gospels of Matthew, Mark, Luke, and John. I am assuming that readers have at least some knowledge of these Gospels, so won't go into any detail summarizing them as I do with the apocryphal Gospels in this chapter. The only point I should note is that—in line with the overwhelming majority of scholars—I think that Mark wrote first, and that Matthew and Luke both made use of Mark when composing their own Gospels.[1]

The apocryphal Gospels covered in this book are those that scholars usually consider the most significant alternative Gospels. Some of them have also entered wider public debate. *The Da Vinci Code* focuses on the *Gospel of Philip*. Dawkins, quoted earlier, mentions the Gospels of Thomas, Peter, and Mary. Christopher Hitchens's book *God Is Not Great* mentions the *Gospel of Mary* and *Gospel of Thomas,* and has a brief discussion of the *Gospel of Judas.*[2] These apocryphal Gospels are all very old—dating from sometime in the second or third centuries. They are also Gospels where we have a good idea of what their main aims and themes are. The exception is the *Gospel of Mary,* which only survives in quite small fragments. Most experts think that the seven apocryphal Gospels that I'm going to look at here originated in or around the second century CE, although—just to be clear—no scholars really think that the apostles Peter and Thomas and Philip and Judas and Mary Magdalene really wrote these Gospels.[3] In fact, in most cases, we don't know who wrote them.

1. Marcion's Gospel

There's only one apocryphal Gospel of which we do know the author's name: Marcion's Gospel. Marcion was a teacher active around 150 CE, and he thought that the wider church was fundamentally wrong about Jesus and the Bible; in reality, Marcion believed, the Old Testament was not about the true or highest God but was only about the evil creator god of the Jews. The New Testament, on the other hand, was about a different deity altogether, the Father of Jesus. But according to Marcion, New Testament books had unfortunately been corrupted by Christians who thought that Jesus was Jewish and the son of the inferior creator god. As a result, Marcion thought that the contaminated references in Paul and the Gospels to Jesus fulfilling the prophecies of this lower god and carrying out acts of judgment needed to be removed. So Marcion produced a very short New Testament, containing a collection of Paul's letters minus what he saw as the deceptive expansions, and a "purified" version of Luke's Gospel. He edited this Gospel around 150 CE, and, although we don't have a manuscript of it, we know a lot from other writers about which parts of Luke's Gospel he kept in and which parts he cut out. For example, having removed Luke's account of the birth of Jesus, Marcion's Gospel starts with Jesus descending from heaven and landing (fully grown) in Galilee.

Sample Extract: The Beginning of Marcion's Gospel

In the fifteenth year of the principate of Tiberius Caesar, in the time of Pontius Pilate, Jesus came down to Capernaum, a town in Gal-

> ilee, and taught there in the synagogue. The people were amazed at his teaching, because his word had such authority. In the synagogue there was a man with the spirit of an unclean demon.
>
> "Leave me alone!" he shrieked. "What do you want with us, Jesus of Nazareth? Have you come to destroy us? I know who you are—the Holy One of God!"
>
> "Be quiet!" Jesus rebuked him. "Come out of him!" The demon threw the man down in their midst, and came out leaving him unharmed.[4]

2. The Valentinian Gospels: The *Gospel of Truth* and the *Gospel of Philip*

A rough contemporary of Marcion in the middle of the second century was another teacher, Valentinus. His followers, who produced the *Gospel of Truth* and the *Gospel of Philip*, were somewhere between an intellectual philosophical academy and a church. Valentinian thought partially overlaps with Marcion's teaching, but it's hard to know whether one influenced the other, because they were operating around the same time. Like Marcion, Valentinus also thought that this world was not created by the supreme God but by a deity lower down in the heavenly hierarchy. As the Valentinian *Gospel of Philip* puts it: "The world came into being by a mistake. For its creator wanted to make it imperishable and immortal, but failed, and he did not achieve what he had hoped" (*Gos. Phil.* 99). The creator made the cosmos without the permission of the supreme deity, and so this world does not have a firm grip on reality but deceives people away from the truth about God and human beings. So, living in the world is like living in the Matrix, with only occasional glitches allowing insight into heavenly truth and into the superior realms of divinity for those who are initiated into the hidden Valentinian understanding. The fundamental plight of human beings is ignorance of who they really are. Jesus, the Son of the divine Father, is the savior figure like in more conventional forms of Christianity, although in the *Gospel of Philip* and the *Gospel of Truth* salvation involves receiving fullness (the solution to deficiency) and knowledge (the solution to ignorance). As one Valentinian theologian defined this knowledge: "It is not washing (in baptism) on its own that sets free, but knowledge: who we were, what we have become, where we were, where we have been thrown, where we are hastening to, from what we are redeemed, what birth is, what rebirth is."[5] The *Gospel of Truth* and the *Gospel of Philip* fit broadly in with this Valentinian theology.

The *Gospel of Truth* is actually a book with some literary style, unlike some apocryphal Gospels that appear to relish convoluted detail. It is structured almost like a Greek myth and tells a story, beginning with the Father, the supreme divinity, who is incomprehensible because he is so far above all other reality. Because of the Father's total separation from anything else, people can't know him, and hence a savior is required to bring back the spirit of the chosen disciples into the Father, who is their true origin and home.

Sample Extract: The Beginning of the *Gospel of Truth*

> The gospel of truth is a joy for those who have received from the Father of truth the gift of knowing him by the power of the Word who has come from the fullness in the Father's thought and intellect. This Word is called "Savior," referring to the name of the work which he was to carry out for the redemption of those who did not know the Father. The term "gospel" means "the revelation of hope." It is a discovery for those who seek him.
>
> Since the All sought after the one from whom it had come forth, and the All had been within the uncontainable and inconceivable one who surpasses all thought, ignorance of the Father brought about turmoil and fear. Now turmoil condensed like a mist, such that no one was able to see. For this reason, Error became powerful, and she worked upon her own matter in vain. Not knowing

the truth, she assumed a form which powerfully manufactured an attractive substitute for the truth.

The *Gospel of Philip* comes in a very different form, as a collection of disconnected and highly symbolic sentences rather than a story. It explains how this world is a confusing, misleading realm, unless—as in the *Gospel of Truth*—you have a Valentinian teacher to interpret reality for you. If you understand it correctly, you will see that this world below contains shards of truth that can be used to understand the heavenly realms. For example, the temple in Jerusalem is an image of the spiritual sanctuary above, sex is a picture of the heavenly bridal chamber in which God and human spirits are united, and circumcision is a metaphor for the removal of a person's sinful nature. On their own, these earthly signs are distorted, because demonic forces have hidden their true meaning. But if you have a Valentinian code-breaker to help, you can understand these earthly symbols and see beyond them into the spiritual realm.

Sample Extract: The Beginning of the *Gospel of Philip*

A Hebrew makes Hebrews, and those of this sort are called "proselytes." A proselyte, however, cannot make proselytes. [. . .]

The slave seeks only to be free. He does not seek his master's property. The son, however, not only is a son but also collects the inheritance from his father after him.

Those who inherit from the dead are themselves dead and inherit what is dead. Those who inherit from the living are alive and inherit what is living along with what is dead. Those who are dead do not inherit anything, for how could a dead person inherit? But if a dead person inherits from the living, he will not die: that dead person will have life in greater abundance.

A gentile does not die, for he has never lived such that he could die. The one who has believed in the truth has received life, and is at risk of dying because he is alive.

3. The Gnostic Gospels: The *Gospel of the Egyptians* and the *Gospel of Judas*

Even more radical than the Valentinians were the Gnostics. Although "Gnostic" is sometimes used as a shorthand for almost anything heretical, in fact in the ancient world it had a particular theological meaning.[6] Those who called themselves Gnostics differed both from orthodox Christians and from Greek philosophers, and both followers of Jesus and followers of Plato wrote books opposing these Gnostics. One Platonist philosopher wrote a work called "Against the Gnostics," which had an alternative title: "Against those who declare the creator of the world and the world itself both to be evil." Naturally this book title is only a short summary of two beliefs about Gnostic thought, which was in fact much more complicated. But it shows that the Gnostics differed from mainstream Christians who believed the creator was supremely good, but also from the Valentinians who believed that the creator was more incompetent than evil. Clearly, this movement or collection of groups was highly subversive in its thought, and the Gnostic books that survive are often critical of Jewish and Christian theology. The Gnostic *Apocryphon of John*, for example, criticizes the first five books of the Bible, pointing out Moses's theological misunderstandings. The Coptic *Gospel of the Egyptians*, which we will look at shortly, comments on how neither the Old Testament prophets nor the apostles of Jesus grasped the truth that is announced in the *Egyptian Gospel*. The Gnostic *Gospel of Judas* rejects the mainstream account of Jesus's last days before his crucifixion as well as the New Testament Gospels' understanding of who Jesus is.

This *Gospel of Judas* only came to public attention in 2006, and so it is one of the "newest" apocryphal Gospels. This Gnostic work originally comes from some time in the middle of the second century. As the title suggests, its most surprising feature is that Judas Iscariot becomes the special recipient of Jesus's revelations. These mysteries that Jesus secretly discloses to Judas are the focus of the book and are very negative about conventional Christian theology. Early on in the *Gospel of Judas*, Jesus mocks the disciples' celebration of the Eucharist, and the apostles are condemned as murderous and sexually deviant priests.

There are two main points in Jesus's revelations to Judas. First, the story is told of how the supreme being, "the Great Invisible Spirit," spawns further spiritual beings in the upper echelons of the realms of the gods. Second, demonic forces make a cosmos below as a copy of the "Cosmos" above, and along with it generate Adam and Eve. As in some other apocryphal Gospels, the goal for true disciples is to get beyond material reality and gain knowledge about the soul. These specially revealed mysteries are the path to salvation, and noticeably the Gospel ends with Judas making a bargain with the chief priests and scribes and delivering Jesus to them. So the book finishes before there is any account of the death and resurrection of Jesus.

Sample Extract: Jesus's First Appearance in the *Gospel of Judas*

> One day in Judaea, Jesus came to the disciples and found them sitting together practicing their piety. When he met them sitting together and giving thanks over the bread, he laughed.
>
> "Master," the disciples asked, "why are you laughing at our thanksgiving? Or is it right what we are doing?"
>
> "I am not laughing at you," Jesus answered. "You are not doing this by your own will, but because your god receives praise from it."
>
> "Master," they said, "you are the son of our god!"
>
> "How do you know me?" Jesus asked them. "Truly, I say to you, no generation of the people in your midst can know me."
>
> When his disciples heard this, they were annoyed and angry, and blasphemed him in their hearts.
>
> When Jesus saw their stupidity, he said to them, "Why this angry agitation? Your god who is within you and [...] annoyed with

> your souls. If any of you is strong, bring forth the perfect man and stand before me."
>
> "We are strong enough," they all replied. But none of their spirits was bold enough to stand in his presence, except that of Judas Iscariot. He was able to stand before Jesus, though not to look into his eyes, and so he turned his face away.
>
> "I know who you are and from where you have come," Judas said to him. "You have come from the immortal aeon of Barbelo! But I am not worthy to utter the name of him who sent you."

Close in theology to the *Gospel of Judas* is the *Gospel of the Egyptians,* also known as the *Holy Book of the Great Invisible Spirit.* This is, frankly, a rather baffling book. It begins with the generation of a bewildering array of deities who come into being as part of the heavenly bureaucracy, again beginning with the Great Invisible Spirit, who gives birth to a trinity of Father, Mother, and Son. Then each of these in turn unfolds other deities in a way that is strongly influenced by Egyptian mythology. The book then describes how the demonic realm emerges and recounts how a divine "Seth" comes to earth to rescue his spiritual seed. This Seth brings salvation by becoming fused with the person of Jesus. Overall, though, Jesus plays only a minor role in the grand myth. The last section of the *Gospel of the Egyptians* sets out the ritual incantations to be followed during baptisms, such as "IE IEUS EO OU EO OUA—verily, verily! O Yesseus Mazareus Yessedekeus," or "AEE Ē Ē Ē III UUUUUU ŌŌŌŌŌŌŌŌ—existent for ever and ever—verily true!" A conclusion describes how Seth himself composed the Gospel, taking 130 years to write it—a surprisingly long time for a book that is hardly a literary masterpiece. It was really written probably around 200 CE.

As in other Gnostic texts, the goal of salvation in the *Gospel of the Egyptians* is not the redemption of the world but total liberation from the material realm, which—like its creators—is evil. The salvation of the individual involves both receiving knowledge and taking part in the ritual practices that are set out at the end of the Gospel.

Sample Extract:
The Beginning of the *Gospel of the Egyptians*

The Holy Book of the Egyptians, the Book of the Great Invisible Spirit, the unnameable Father, who is from the heights, who is the perfect light, the eternal light of the aeons; light in the silence in the Providence and silence of the Father; light in word and truth; light incorruptible; light unbounded; the radiance from the aeons of the light of the invisible, untraceable, ageless, unproclaimable Father; aeon of the aeons; self-generated, self-generating, self-emanating; the stranger; uninterpretable power of the ineffable Father. From him came forth three powers—the Father, the Mother and the Son—from themselves, from the living silence, the radiance from the incorruptible Father. They came forth from the silence of the unseen Father.

From that place there came forth Domedon Doxomedon, the aeon of the aeons and the light of each of their powers. In this way, the Son emanated fourth, the Mother fifth, and the Father sixth. He was unknown, untraceable among all the powers and incorruptible glories.

4. The *Gospel of Peter*

With the *Gospel of Peter* we escape the ethereal Gnostic mysteries and return to planet earth. Like Marcion's Gospel and the New Testament Gospels, the *Gospel of Peter* tells a story of Jesus's ministry. The long fragment that survives covers the death and resurrection of Jesus, although originally the book as a whole was probably a full-length Gospel, beginning with Jesus's birth or baptism. The *Gospel of Peter* is noteworthy because it is the only example of an apocryphal Gospel we know to have been read out in a church (in Rhossus in Syria), at least for a short time, alongside the canonical Gospels. It was probably written sometime around 150–180 CE.

Although it has a lot in common with the New Testament accounts of Jesus's death and resurrection, there are three features of the *Gospel of Peter* that stand out. First, in the account of the crucifixion, Jesus is entirely silent except for the words spoken at the moment he dies: "*My power, O power, you have abandoned me*" (*Gos. Pet.* 5:19). Second, when he rises from the dead, Jesus's resurrected body is gigantic, towering above heaven itself. Jesus walks out of his tomb accompanied by a talking cross that gives verbal confirmation that Jesus after his crucifixion went down to the underworld and preached to the souls of the dead there (see the extract below). Third, the *Gospel of Peter* also differs in tone from the canonical Gospels, and has a clear anti-Jewish emphasis: the actions of the Roman soldiers in the canonical portrayals of Jesus's crucifixion are, in the *Gospel of Peter*, all transferred to Jews: the decision to execute Jesus, the mockery, the presentation of the crown of thorns and of the vinegary drink, and the crucifixion itself. As a result, a curse comes over Judea and upon the Jewish people, according to this Gospel.

Sample Extract: The Resurrection Scene in the *Gospel of Peter*

During the following night in which the Lord's Day dawned, as the soldiers were guarding two by two on duty, there was a great voice in the sky. The soldiers saw the heavens opened and two men coming down from there, in brilliant light, approaching the tomb. The stone which had been placed at the entrance rolled away of its own accord and made some space for them to enter. Since the tomb was open, both the young men went in.

When the soldiers saw this, they woke up the centurion and the elders who were also on guard there. As they were explaining what they had seen, they saw three men coming out from the tomb, two of them holding the other one aloft, and a cross following behind them. The heads of the two reached up to heaven, but the head of the one carried along by them went up beyond the heavens. Then those present heard a voice from the heavens.

"Have you preached to those who are asleep?"
"Yes!" came the answer from the cross.

5. The *Gospel of Thomas*

Not to be confused with the *Infancy Gospel of Thomas,* which is an account of Jesus's childhood, this other *Gospel of Thomas* is a kind of a database of Jesus's teaching. It was probably written sometime between 140 and 180 CE. The book is a mixture of pithy sayings (like "Become passers-by!") and parables (like a version of the parable of the sower) as well as dialogues between Jesus and his male and female disciples. About half of the collection is familiar from the canonical Gospels, while the other half is a compilation of more esoteric teaching. The most striking saying perhaps is the finale, in which Jesus promises to make Mary Magdalene male so that she can enter the kingdom of heaven.

The main theme of the *Gospel of Thomas* is the unique revelation of the divine that Jesus unveils. This revelation contains the sacred "knowledge" that is a major theme in the Gospel. (In contrast to one reference to faith, there are thirty-two references to "knowledge" or "understanding.") This knowledge leads to a transformation that can separate disciples from the material body and the physical world, and can reunite them with their true spiritual origin in Jesus. In response to Jesus's disclosure of the truth, disciples of *Thomas*'s Jesus must master the content of this revealed truth and understand its hidden meaning. This is the true path to salvation and immortality, as the opening of the book shows.

Sample Extract: The Beginning of the *Gospel of Thomas*

These are the secret sayings which the living Jesus spoke, and Didymus Judas Thomas wrote them down.

Jesus said, "Whoever finds the interpretation of these sayings will not taste death."

Jesus said, "He who seeks should not stop seeking until he finds. When he finds, he will be troubled, and when he is troubled, he will be astonished, and will reign over the All."

Jesus said, "If those who lead you say to you, 'Behold, the kingdom is in heaven,' then the birds of heaven would precede you! If they say to you, 'It is in the sea,' then the fish would precede you! No, the kingdom is inside you and outside you. When you know yourselves, you will be known and will understand that you are sons of the living Father. But if you do not know yourselves, you live in poverty and you are poverty."

6. The *Gospel of Mary*

Finally, a brief mention of the *Gospel of Mary*—the Mary here being Mary Magdalene, not the mother of Jesus. Unfortunately, this *Gospel of Mary* is very poorly preserved, with only small fragments of it surviving. We have less than half of what is already a short text, and crucially we are missing the first six pages. As a result, it is very hard to get a sense of its overall theology. So the rest of this book will not attempt to compare the thinking of the *Gospel of Mary* with the other works covered here, because it would be unfair to judge this Gospel given that we know so little of the original text.

As far as we can tell, the *Gospel of Mary* has some themes in common with Gnostic or Valentinian thought, even though this Gospel may not have derived from either of those movements. The most obviously striking element of the *Gospel of Mary* is its claim to come from a female disciple. Originally written in Greek in the second century CE, the fragments that survive have two main features. First, in a dialogue between Mary and the male disciples, Peter asks Mary to reveal what Jesus secretly taught her. When he hears what she has to say, though, Peter then seems to change his mind. He and his brother Andrew doubt whether Jesus would really have taught a woman anything that he had not taught the male disciples. Mary is upset by this, but the apostle Levi jumps to her defense and criticizes Peter's misogyny. In the end, Levi and Mary prevail, and the disciples go forth as a united front to preach the good news. Second, the main theological theme of the surviving text, which comes in a vision given to Mary, is how the soul can pass hostile powers on its way up to heaven and reach the supreme God. This motif appears in lots of apocryphal books and is perhaps influenced by Egyptian mythology. Here in the *Gospel of Mary*, though, the powers are not external demonic forces that need to be thwarted but apparently personifications of a person's sinful tendencies—like "Desire" and "Ignorance." The presence of Jesus is clearly implied in the book, although he is not named: he is usually called "the savior" or "Lord," and at one point is referred to as an incarnation of "the Good," the supreme form or idea in Plato's thought.

Sample Extract from the *Gospel of Mary*

"Sister," Peter said to Mary, "we know that the Savior loved you more than any other woman. Tell us the Savior's words as you remember them—those which you know but which we haven't heard."

"What you missed but which I remember," Mary replied, "I will declare to you." So she began telling them the words.

"Once I saw the Lord in a vision and I spoke to him:

"'Lord, this very day I have seen you in a vision!'

"'You are blessed,' he answered me, 'because you did not waver when you saw me! For where the intellect is, there the treasure is.'

"'O Lord,' I said, 'does the person who now sees a vision see himself by the soul or by the spirit?'

"'He does not see by the soul or by the spirit,' the Savior replied. 'It is the intellect which is between them which sees the vision.'"

. . .

[Mary recounts her vision of the holy soul ascending to heaven.]

"Desire said, 'I did not see you descending, but now I can see you ascending! How can you lie to me when you belong to me?'

"'I saw you,' the soul answered, 'though you did not see me or recognize me. To you I was only a garment and you did not know me.'

"When it had finished speaking, the soul went on with much rejoicing.

"Then it reached the third power, called 'Ignorance.' That power also interrogated the soul.

"'Where are you trying so wickedly to go? You are under arrest! You are under arrest to face judgement!'

"'Why do you judge me, when I have not judged?' the soul said. 'And why am I under arrest when I have arrested no one? I have not been recognized, but I recognize the dissolution of the All, both its earthly and its heavenly parts.'

"After the soul had defeated the third power, it ascended.

"Then it saw the fourth power which had seven forms: The first form was Darkness, the second Desire, the third Ignorance, the fourth Death's Jealousy, the fifth Flesh's Kingdom, the sixth Flesh's Foolish 'Understanding,' the seventh Angry Wisdom. These were the seven wrathful powers which interrogate the soul.

"'From where have you come, you murderer?' they asked. 'And where are you going, you world-destroyer?'

"'What arrested me has been slain,' the soul replied, 'and what surrounded me has been defeated. My desire has come to an end and my ignorance has perished. By a world I have been released from a world, and by a heavenly form from a form and from the temporary fetter of oblivion. From now on, I can receive the silent rest that belongs to the course of the Aeon's time.'"

When Mary had finished speaking, she fell silent, since that was all that the Savior had spoken.

"Brethren," Andrew replied, "what do you think about what she has said? I for one don't believe that the Savior said all that! After all, it is in quite a different vein from his thinking."

Conclusion

These Gospels are obviously not all the same and don't make up some kind of alternative canon. Some are Gnostic, others Valentinian, one is Marcionite, and the others can't easily be assigned to a particular group. They don't agree with each other theologically but represent facets of the diversity of second-century Christianity and provide different windows into how a variety of different people understood the figure of Jesus at that time. What they are all attempting to do, just like the New Testament Gospels, is to present the good news about Jesus: the word "gospel" simply means "good news." The claim to write a "good news" book is a claim to present the gospel message of how Jesus has brought salvation. The rest of this book, though, aims to show that there are important ways in which these apocryphal Gospels all differ from the four New Testament Gospels, which are united in their thinking about Jesus and the good news.

CHAPTER TWO

How Do You Tell Gospels Apart?

Now that we have begun to survey this large field of various Gospels, can we say that there is any difference between the New Testament Gospels and the others? Some think that the selection was almost arbitrary, as Richard Dawkins says in the quotation in the introduction. For some scholars it was not arbitrary but instead a careful political power play, in which bishops imposed their Gospels on the common Christians, excommunicated the heretics, and burned any books that did not meet official approval.

If the selection wasn't arbitrary or just political, is there anything that differentiates between the New Testament Gospels and the non-canonical or "apocryphal" Gospels? To decide this, we will have to take a step back and think about the various ways we might compare all these Gospels with each other.

1. Normality?

One of the most popular ways of comparing the biblical Gospels with others is to judge according to normality, that is, the New Testament Gospels are fairly normal while the apocryphal ones are "strange." One author, for example, describes a miracle in the *Infancy Gospel* as containing "the weird story about Jesus making twelve sparrows out of mud."[1] Certainly there are surprising and unusual statements in the apocrypha. The *Gospel of Thomas* concludes with this dialogue:

> "Mary should leave us," Simon Peter said, "because women are not worthy of life."
>
> "Now I will draw her to me to make her male," Jesus said, "to make her a living spirit resembling you males. For every woman who makes herself male will enter the kingdom of heaven." (*Gos. Thom.* 114)

In this dialogue, Peter's view is downright sexist and chauvinistic, although Jesus's reply is not exactly #MeToo either.

But before we rush to write the apocrypha off as unusual, we should probably stop and remember how the New Testament Gospels can be rather "weird" as well. Jesus may not have used mud to make sparrows, but he did mix mud with his saliva and put the concoction on the eyes of a man to cure his blindness (John 9:1–6). Some of the episodes in the Gospels have really baffled readers down the centuries. Matthew writes, for example: "Just then the curtain of the temple was torn in two from top to bottom. The earth shook, the rocks split, and the tombs broke open. The bodies of many holy people who had died were raised to life. They came out of the tombs after Jesus' resurrection, and went into the holy city and appeared to many people" (Matt 27:51–53).[2] According to this passage, Jesus's crucifixion resuscitated a lot of Old Testament saints, who then stayed in their tombs for three days, and afterward went wandering around Jerusalem.

Jesus's teachings in the Gospels can also be strange. He tells people to sell all their possessions but also to buy a sword if they don't have one, to love their neighbors but hate their parents, and teaches that some people are apparently saved by faith but others need to keep the commandments to win eternal life. He even tells people to be perfect as God is perfect.[3]

The problem with comparing biblical and apocryphal Gospels on the basis of their reasonableness or oddness is that these criteria are quite subjective. Are there ways of comparing the Gospels that are more rooted in history rather than in our own standards of what's normal?

2. Authorship

One standard way of distinguishing between canonical and non-canonical Gospels is by who wrote them. This goes back to the ancient church. When the church father Tertullian writes against the Gospel of Marcion in around 200 CE, he has this to say about the four New Testament Gospels: "I lay it down to begin with that the documents of the gospel have the apostles for their authors, and that this task of publishing the gospel was imposed upon them by our Lord himself."[4] So Jesus instructed his disciples to write the Gospels, and they then fulfilled that commission. Another church father, Cyril of Jerusalem, lays down a reason why no Christian should look at apocryphal Gospels: "Let no one read the Gospel according to Thomas. For it is not from one of the twelve apostles, but from one of the three evil disciples of Mani."[5] Cyril's main point here is the negative one: the author of this Gospel wasn't an apostle. This is a fairly conventional argument made by church fathers at that time. As Tertullian commented, the Gospels were written by the apostles of Christ on the authority of Christ.

But even on the traditional view that Matthew, Mark, Luke, and John wrote the Gospels, there is a slight wrinkle in the argument for apostolic authorship: only Matthew and John were apostles or disciples of Jesus; Mark and Luke weren't. Tertullian recognizes this. He distinguishes between "apostles" and "apostolics," and Mark and Luke belong to this second category—they weren't apostles but were only apostle-ish! They qualified as apostolic because they were closely connected to apostles—Mark was a disciple of Peter, and Luke was a companion of Paul.[6] So if the Gospels were a product of apostolic authorship, they are only this in a broad sense. They are not all written by apostles.

A further complication is that many scholars do not even think that Matthew, Mark, Luke, and John wrote the Gospels at all. These commentators reckon that the Gospels were originally anonymous, and the names of the Gospel authors were only added later. Although this is implausible,[7] there is a strong contingent of scholarship that sees the canonical Gospels and the apocryphal Gospels as essentially the same as far as authorship is concerned: they are all in the same unapostolic boat.

3. Dating

Related to the question of authorship is the question of when the Gospels were written. Already at the end of the second century, Bishop Irenaeus attacks the *Gospel of Truth* on the grounds that it was only recently written, in contrast to the canonical Gospels, which have been handed down from the time of the apostles.[8] Around the same time, one early document discussing which books belong in the New Testament comments that the *Shepherd of Hermas* was written "very recently, in our times."[9] Early church theologians often assumed that, as Tertullian puts it, "the greater claim to truth is what is earlier, and what is earlier is what has also been so since the beginning."[10]

Similarly, some modern scholars defend the New Testament Gospels on the grounds that they were the earliest, written in the first century, in contrast to the apocryphal Gospels, which came from the second. Most scholars agree that this is probably true, but on the other hand, the distance in time between the first century and the second century is a nonexistent moment. More reasonable is the claim that the first century roughly corresponds to the period during which eyewitnesses such as Jesus's disciples and family were alive, whereas by the second century almost all of Jesus's contemporaries were dead.

4. Biographical Narration

Another way in which some have compared Gospels is to focus on how the New Testament versions are narratives, or stories. After all, they give a sequential biography of Jesus. Mark starts from the beginning of Jesus's ministry, Matthew and Luke open with his birth, and John goes back deep into eternity past. And they extend, via descriptions of Jesus's mighty words and mighty deeds, right up to his resurrection. In short, the Gospels contain what the beginning of Acts calls "everything which Jesus began to do and to teach" (Acts 1:1).

By contrast, as noted in the previous chapter, the *Gospel of Thomas* is a database of 114 sayings with no real action. Similarly, the *Gospel of Philip* consists of a similar number of enigmatic sayings and short discourses. The *Gospel of Judas* has tidbits of narrative, but it only starts about three days before the crucifixion. And those final days of Jesus contain no narration of Jesus's trials and sufferings but only his announcements of how the divine realm above is full of myriads of angels, deities, luminaries, heavens, spirits, aeons, immortals, and firmaments.

As a result of this, some have argued that these noncanonical texts shouldn't really be called Gospels at all. They contain "advice," not "news."[11] And news is what Gospels should be about. Our English term "gospel" comes from the Old English words *god/godd* (good) and *spel/spell* (news). This matches the original Greek word, *euangelion*: the *eu-* part means "good" or "well," and the *-angelion* part means "message" or "announcement."

But the problem with distinguishing between canonical and noncanonical Gospels on the basis of whether they're biographies or not is that this doesn't work for a number of the apocryphal Gospels: several of them are in fact narratives of Jesus's life as well. Marcion's Gospel is a biographical narrative, beginning with Jesus descending from heaven to Capernaum in his thirtieth year. So is the *Diatessaron,* a mega-Gospel combining all four canonical Gospels into one. There is also a *Gospel of the Hebrews,* which extends at least from Jesus's baptism and up to his resurrection, as well as a *Gospel of the Ebionites,* which is a sequential story. The *Gospel of Peter* is also a narrative, probably beginning with Jesus's childhood and certainly extending to his resurrection. So there is no hard-and-fast distinction between narrative New Testament Gospels and apocryphal Gospels that take other forms.

5. Popularity?

Scholars have also tried to work out which of the Gospels were the most popular in the early church, especially in the second and third centuries. This early phase was when Gospels started to be copied extensively by scribes and quoted by other authors. If we look at the evidence from the first 200–250 years of the church, it's clear that

Christians copied New Testament books much more than they did apocryphal books. The most popular Gospels by quite a long way were those of Matthew and John, partly because they were apostles. Matthew and John were so dominant that there were relatively few copies of Mark (most of which is incorporated into Matthew's Gospel anyway). Before about 300 CE, there are roughly the same number of manuscripts of Mark as of the *Gospel of Peter* and the *Gospel of Thomas*—two of Mark, one or two of *Peter*, but three of *Thomas.*

On the other hand, if we look at how often other authors quoted or referred to the Gospels, the canonical versions come out on top by a long way. If we take two early authors who knew a wide range of literature, we see a clear divide in the authors they value. Saint Irenaeus, who was bishop of Lyon in France, wrote a large five-volume work on heresies in his day. He quotes the canonical Gospels hundreds of times but refers to others—the *Gospel of Judas* and *Gospel of Truth,* and possibly the *Gospel of Thomas* and *Infancy Gospel of Thomas*—on only a handful of occasions. Similarly, the great Christian scholar Clement of Alexandria was writing at about the same time as Irenaeus but hundreds of miles away in Egypt. His pattern of quoting authorities was about the same as Irenaeus, however: he also refers to Matthew, Mark, Luke, and John a vast number of times but has only a few references to the *Gospel of the Egyptians,* the *Gospel of the Hebrews,* and the *Gospel of Matthias.*

But there's a danger of a vicious circle here. Of course Bishop Irenaeus is going to quote the four New Testament Gospels a lot more than the heretical Gospels he is arguing against: it's a big part of his argument that there are four, and only four, Gospels. "*The Gospels could not possibly be either more or less in number than they are,*" he wrote.[12] And Clement of Alexandria would do the same: he is also an advocate for orthodoxy as well. In any case, truth is not necessarily measured by the majority!

6. Differences of Theological Message

This book is going to argue that a central difference between the canonical Gospels and the best-known apocryphal Gospels on the other lies in their *theologies*. This approach also has a long pedigree. Bishop Irenaeus in the second century commented that the *Gospel of Truth* was "completely different" from the canonical Gospels handed down.[13] Later, the fourth-century theologian Eusebius comments on various noncanonical Gospels that are "un-apostolic in character" both in their messages and in the ways the authors express those messages.[14]

As we saw in the section on "Biographical Narration" earlier, there was a particular reason why certain books in the ancient world were called "Gospels." In ancient Greek and Latin literature, there were tragedies, comedies, histories, and novels. In the Old Testament, there are collections of hymns and proverbs, as well as historical books and prophecy. In varying degrees, all literature has a message. What is different about a Gospel—whether inside or outside the New Testament—is that it doesn't just *contain* a message. It *is* a message. The English word "gospel"—like its Greek equivalent *euangelion*—means "good *news*." Part of the essence of a preached *euangelion* or a written *euangelion* is that it is an announcement. This book is going to focus on how the various Gospels treat the original Christian message.

Conclusion

The point here is not that all these other methods of distinguishing between canonical and noncanonical Gospels are invalid. Scholars have written whole books arguing about the dating of the various Gospels, or about how the New Testament Gospels uniquely contain biographical narration.[15] My focus here in this short book is on comparing the theological messages of the various Gospels. This approach will be fleshed out more in the next chapter.

CHAPTER THREE

Comparing Gospel Messages

How do we compare the messages of different Gospels? There are so many aspects of their messages we could compare: these Gospels' understandings of the church, their positions on "the last things," or how they thought Christians should live, to take just a few examples. We could engage in dozens of comparisons of early Christian Gospels, finding all sorts of points in common and points of divergence among them. There is a joke that goes: What do Winnie the Pooh and Alexander the Great have in common? This is a fairly baffling sort of comparison; the answer to the question is: they have the same middle name. What they have in common is, as we might expect, something completely trivial.

How do we know which similarities and differences between Gospels are important and which are trivial? The aim here is to use the early Christian good news preached by the apostles as the way to assess the similarities and differences among all these early Christian Gospels. The reason for using this particular criterion is that the apostolic-preached gospel is undoubtedly an important theme—indeed, the most important theme in earliest Christianity. By using the apostolic good news as a yardstick, we will have an ancient and weighty way to distinguish between Gospels that do follow the message of Jesus's disciples and those that don't.

1. The Shared Gospel Message of the Apostles

One place where the New Testament articulates that apostolic preached gospel comes in 1 Corinthians 15:

> [1]Brothers and sisters, let me remind you of the gospel I preached to you, which you received and on which you have taken your stand. [2]By this gospel you are saved, if you hold firmly to the word I preached to you. Otherwise, you have believed in vain. [3]For what I received I passed on to you as of first importance: that Christ died for our sins according to the Scriptures, [4]that he was buried, that he was raised on the third day according to the Scriptures, [5]and that he appeared to Cephas, and then to the Twelve. [6]After that, he appeared to more than five hundred of the brothers and sisters on a single occasion, most of whom are still alive, although some have fallen asleep. [7]Then he appeared to James, and then to all the apostles. [8]Last of all he appeared to me as well, as to one abnormally born. [9]For I am the least of the apostles, not even deserving to be called an apostle, because I persecuted the church of God. [10]But by the grace of God I am what I am, and his grace to me was not without effect. No, I worked harder than all of them—yet not I, but the grace of God that was with me. [11]Therefore, whether it is I or they, this is what we preach, and this is what you believed. (1 Cor 15:1–11)

Especially in verses 3–5, we have a summary here of what the apostles preached. Paul notes in verse 11 that "they"—the other apostles—preach the same good news that Paul and the Corinthians possess. He lists these others as Cephas, a.k.a. Peter (v. 5), James the brother of Jesus (v. 7), and the Twelve, as well as other "apostles" in the loose sense of "missionaries"—people like Barnabas, who is called an apostle in the book of Acts.[1]

In this passage, Paul underlines how central this message is:

- It is the *gospel*, the good news (v. 1).
- It is what Paul himself received (v. 3a).

- It is what Paul then proclaimed (literally, "gospelled") to the Corinthians (v. 1).
- It is what the Corinthians believed (v. 2b; cf. v. 11).
- It was how they are saved (v. 2a).
- It is the most important message in the world (v. 3a).
- It is the message that all the apostles preach (v. 11).

This last point is a very important one. Paul is not talking about his private gospel; no, it is the gospel message or good news common to all Jesus's disciples. However unusual Paul was, he shared the same gospel message with the other apostolic leaders in early Christianity.

2. The Ingredients of the Apostles' Message of the Good News

The core of this message comes in verses 3b–5: "Christ died for our sins according to the Scriptures, that he was buried, that he was raised on the third day according to the Scriptures, and that he appeared to Cephas, and then to the Twelve." Here we can pick out the four key elements of this message:

2.1. Jesus as the "Christ"/"Messiah"

There were actually hundreds of people in the ancient world called "Jesus." In the Old Testament, the Hebrew "Joshua" is equivalent to our "Jesus": Hebrew *Yehoshua* becomes Greek *Iesous,* which becomes Latin *Iesus,* which becomes English *Jesus.* There are four Joshuas/Jesuses in the Old Testament, another one in Jesus's genealogy (Luke 3:29), and two other minor Jesus characters in the New Testament—Jesus Barabbas and Jesus Justus (Matt 27:16–17; Col 4:11). As far as we can tell from literature and documents of the time, in the New Testament period Jesus was the sixth-most-popular name for Jewish men (after Simon, Joseph, Eleazar, Judah, and John).[2]

The central fact about the most important Jesus for the early Christians was that he was the *Christ.* "Christ" isn't a surname but a title with crucial significance. As time went on, some people would treat Christ just as a name, but at the beginning it certainly wasn't. The Greek word *Christos,* the New Testament word we translate as Christ, was actually a rare Greek word, and to call someone *Christos* would sound very odd. Here's the very technical definition of *Christos* (χριστός) in the most widely used dictionary of ancient Greek:

> χριστός, ή, όν, (χρίω) ***to be rubbed on,*** **used as *ointment* or *salve,***
> opp. πιστός, A.Pr.480, cf. E.Hipp.516, Triclin.ad Theoc.11.1;
> τὸ ἔλαιον τὸ χ. anointing oil, LXX Le.21.10.
> II. of persons, anointed, ὁ ἱερεύς ὁ χ. ib.4.5,16, 6.22: pl., ib.2 Ma.1.10.
> 2. esp. of the Kings of Israel, ὁ χ. Κυρίου ib.1 Ki.24.7, cf. Ps.17 (18).51;
> also τῷ χ. μου Κύρῳ Is.45.1; pl., of the patriarchs, Ps.104 (105).15.
> 3. in NT, ὁ χ. the Messiah, Ev.Matt.2.4, etc.; ὁ χ. Κυρίου
> Ev.Luc.2.26; then used as pr. n. of Jesus, Ἰησοῦς χ. Ev.Matt.1.1,
> etc.; Ἰησοῦς ὁ λεγόμενος χ. ib.16.[3]

The key point to notice here is in the first paragraph. "Christ" means "*to be rubbed on,* used as *ointment*"! In that initial definition, we have references to "A.Pr."—the fifth-century BCE play *Prometheus Bound* by Aeschylus, and to "E.Hipp."—Euripides's play *Hippolytus,* from the same period. These dramatists both take something that is a *christos* to be a liquid cure, one which is rubbed on like a cream, not drunk as a potion. The reference after that ("Triclin.ad Theoc.11.1") is a medieval commentary. The next four lines contain Jewish references from the "LXX"—the Greek translation of the Old Testament: the Greek word *christos* appears in this translation as the equivalent of the Hebrew word *meshiach,* or "anointed one." Then finally, in part "3" of the definitions are some illustrative instances from the Gospels.

What that means is that there's a grand total of two pre-Christian, "gentile" references to the word *christos.* And even these two references appear five hundred years before Jesus does. In addition, the fact that both Aeschylus and Euripides clarify that it is a medicine, and contrast it with a potion, may suggest that even to Greek speakers its meaning was unclear. It wasn't a Greek or Latin name either. As a result, the apostles would have had quite a lot of explaining to do: Paul or Peter or John couldn't just get up in front of non-Jews and preach, "The ointment died for your sins." Gentile pagans wouldn't even have had a chance to be offended by the content of the good news, that the Jewish savior had been crucified. They would have failed to understand even what was being said. So the first Christians, encountering any non-Jewish audiences, would have had to explain quite clearly the category of "Christ" or "Messiah." Although it seems like a natural term for us, it was a very strange name or title for an ancient audience.

But who or what was this Messiah? There wasn't a fixed meaning that all Jews everywhere attached to the word, but it was at least a recognizable term. The Messiah was, as the name suggests, "anointed"—that is, commissioned by God for a particular role. In a sense there were lots of "messiahs," including all the Old Testament priests or kings. Nevertheless, many Jews expected a single Messiah figure—*the* Anointed One—to come in the future. He was often expected to be a king equipped with supernatural power to bring about a new golden age of peace and safety for Israel. This might come about because the Messiah had vanquished Israel's enemies, either in a military victory ("with a rod of iron") or by miraculous means ("by the word of his mouth").[4] The essential point was that ancient Jews created a job description for the Messiah by weaving together different Old Testament passages—some authors emphasizing his military might (e.g., from Ps 89), some his descent from David (e.g., from 2 Sam 7), and some his superhuman qualities (e.g., from Dan 7).

Whatever the various Old Testament passages that ancient Jews used to define the Messiah, the first Christians—who were also Jews—were convinced that Jesus fulfilled that job description. As we will see in the next chapter, there is a large range of Old Testament passages used to show how Jesus is the Messiah. Early Christians explained Jesus with lots of different titles and images—the Son of God, the Son of Man, Lord, the great high priest, the lamb, even the Word who was himself God. But the central title was "Christ," and it is this title that is highlighted in the formula "*Christ* died for our sins according to the Scriptures. . . ."

2.2. *Saving Death*

The next important theme in the apostolic gospel captured in 1 Corinthians 15 is "Christ *died for our sins*"—in other words, Jesus's essential saving death. Jesus on the cross carried people's sins and took the consequences. In the Old Testament, the common pattern is that people die as a consequence of their own sins: Adam and Eve in the Garden of Eden transgress God's commandment, and the penalty is "you shall surely die" (Gen 2:16–17). When God gives Israel the law on Mount Sinai, he promises them blessings if they obey and curses if they disregard the law: so Moses addresses them, "I have set before you life and death, blessings and curses" (Deut 30:19). This happens on an individual level as well: King Zimri "*died for his sins* which he had committed" (1 Kgs 16:18–19). This is the standard biblical pattern.

There is an outstanding exception to what happens to people, however, in Isaiah 53:

> Therefore I will give him a portion among the great,
> and he will divide the spoils with the strong,
> because he poured out his life unto death,
> and was numbered with the transgressors.
> For he bore the sin of many,
> and made intercession for the transgressors. (Isa 53:12)

This figure, often known as the "suffering servant," has the opposite destiny to Zimri's. Isaiah describes the servant's life as given over to "death" for sins—though not for his own but for "the sin of many."

This is probably one of the main Old Testament passages that the apostles had in mind when they explained that Christ "died for our sins." In Isaiah 53 the servant, in some mysterious way that history does not record, rescued Israel through his own death. The people later look back and realize what that death had achieved, and that they had misunderstood who the servant was and what he was accomplishing. They had thought that he was cursed by God, "punished by God, stricken by him, and afflicted" (53:4). They later realize, however, that the suffering and death that he endured was their salvation:

> But he was pierced for our transgressions,
>   he was crushed for our iniquities;
> the punishment that brought us peace was on him,
>   and by his wounds we are healed. (Isa 53:5)

In the same way, Jesus's contemporaries hadn't understood who he really was. Some thought Jesus was a deceiver, a demon-possessed magician leading the people astray.[5] Even his own family thought he was mad (Mark 3:21), and his disciples were crushingly disappointed when he was crucified (Luke 24:19–21). However, like the people in Isaiah 53 who come to a delayed recognition of the servant, Jesus's followers and family (and many others) came to a delayed recognition of who Jesus really was. And with that, they understood that Jesus's crucifixion was not a crushing disappointment but instead "the punishment that brought us peace." Jesus's death was the essential means to people's salvation.

2.3. *Jesus's Resurrection*

In fact, it is not quite true that Jesus's death is *the* essential means to people's salvation. To say this would miss a key point: equally important for salvation is Jesus's resurrection. The early Christians didn't just think of the resurrection as the icing on the cake, or a kind of proof that the cross had really worked or that Jesus really was who he said he was. The resurrection itself brings salvation: sharing in Jesus's new life was as important as sharing in his death. When early Christians were baptized, they didn't just stay under the water—they also had to "rise again." That's why the resurrection is part of the gospel "by which you were saved," as Paul says to the Corinthians (1 Cor 15:2). As 1 Peter puts it: “in his great mercy [God] has given us new birth into a living hope through the resurrection of Jesus Christ from the dead” (1 Pet 1:3). Of course, the biblical authors sometimes stress Jesus’s death. Paul says on one occasion: “For I resolved to know nothing while I was with you except Jesus Christ and him crucified” (1 Cor 2:2). On the other hand, though, Luke can write: “Paul was preaching the good news about Jesus and the resurrection” (Acts 17:18). There is no contradiction here. As 1 Corinthians 15 and the gospel narratives make clear, Jesus’s death and resurrection are both equally important.

2.4. *Jesus’s Fulfillment of Scripture*

The fact that this message emphasizes both the cross and the resurrection comes out clearly from the balanced statement:

> Christ died for our sins according to the Scriptures. (1 Cor 15:3)
>
> He was raised on the third day according to the Scriptures. (1 Cor 15:4)

The key point of the repeated phrase “according to the Scriptures” is that the first Easter was—at least in God’s purposes—not a surprise; it did not come out of a clear blue sky but was planned all along. And that plan was encapsulated in the Scriptures.

In a way, the “death-resurrection” pattern is woven throughout the Bible. Joseph is cast down into a pit, and then is elevated to grand vizier of Egypt (Gen 37–50). Israel goes into exile, and then returns (e.g., Isa 40:1–5). Job is afflicted so grievously that he wished he was dead (Job 7:15–16) but then “the Lord restored his fortunes and gave him twice as much as he had before” (42:10). We might be surprised by the order of these descriptions of God:

> “I put to death and I bring to life.” (Deut 32:39)
>
> “The Lord brings death and makes alive;
> he brings down to the grave and raises up.” (1 Sam 2:6)

But these statements capture the fact that God has organized his plan of salvation not by the natural order of birth then death but by a redemptive order of death then new life. The pattern "died . . . raised" in the apostolic gospel is "according to the Scriptures."

In addition to a broad pattern, there are also specific statements which the apostles may have had in mind. Scholars don't struggle to find precursors to Jesus's sacrificial death in the Old Testament, given the whole system of atoning sacrifices along with the Passover ritual, as well as the suffering servant already mentioned. Some do find it difficult to find an Old Testament background to the resurrection, but there is no reason to be skeptical of it. In addition to the larger pattern we have just seen, Jesus had already recognized his resurrection anticipated in one of the psalms:

> "The stone the builders rejected
>   has become the cornerstone;
> the Lord has done this,
>   and it is marvelous in our eyes." (Mark 12:10–11,
>   quoting Ps 118:22–23)

Another example is the case of Jonah: "For as Jonah was three days and three nights in the belly of a huge fish, so the Son of Man will be three days and three nights in the heart of the earth" (Matt 12:40, quoting Jonah 1:17).

One passage where the wording is very close to Paul's Greek in 1 Corinthians comes in the Greek translation of Hosea:

> "Let us go and return to the Lord our God,
>   for he seizes us,
>   but he will heal us;
> he will strike us down,
>   but he will bind us up.
> After two days he will heal us;
>   on the third day, we will rise again,
>   and live in his presence." (Hos 6:1–2 [Greek])

The twin themes of death and resurrection come together again in Isaiah 53:

> After he has suffered,
> he will see the light of life and be satisfied;
> by his knowledge my righteous servant will justify many,
> and he will bear their iniquities.
> Therefore I will give him a portion among the great,
> and he will divide the spoils with the strong,
> because he poured out his life unto death,
> and was numbered with the transgressors. (Isa 53:11–12)

Here again we get the pattern: the servant's life will be "poured out" in death, but "after he has suffered, he will see the light of life." It's easy to imagine how and why both in the general scriptural pattern and in these particular passages like Psalm 118, Jonah 1, Hosea 6, and Isaiah 53 the apostles would have seen Jesus prefigured.

These four components—(1) Jesus as the Christ, (2) his essential saving death, (3) the resurrection, and (4) his fulfillment of Scripture—are the heart of the early Christian message of the apostles. There are other minor elements as well. As we see in 1 Corinthians 15, after the references to Jesus's death and resurrection, there are mentions of his burial and appearances, but these elements are not saving events in themselves; they are subservient to the death and resurrection. The burial confirms that Jesus was really dead; the appearances confirm that he really did rise.

Conclusion and Preview

In the first chapter we examined the *what* of comparison; in other words, the things that we are comparing: the various Gospels, canonical and noncanonical. Now, in this chapter, we have focused on the *how* of comparison; in other words, how we should approach the whole question of how to compare all those various Gospels. In the rest of this book, then, we are going to make a comparison of Matthew, Mark, Luke, John, *Thomas, Peter, Philip, Judas, Egyptians,* the *Gospel of Truth,* and Marcion's Gospel. And the comparison is specifically going to be of how each of those Gospels treats the four elements of the apostolic message: (1) Jesus as the Christ, (2) his saving death, (3) his resurrection on the third day, and (4) his fulfillment of Scripture. Those are the four criteria that are going to be in operation in the comparison.

The aim of this comparison will to be demonstrate the first key claim of this book:

PROPOSITION 1

The four New Testament Gospels share key elements of theological content that mark them out from most of the noncanonical Gospels.

The first part of the argument, then, is that the four New Testament Gospels share a common affirmation of the four components of the apostolic good news. By contrast, the apocryphal Gospels are silent, selective, or in outright disagreement about them.

There is a second argument following on from this:

PROPOSITION 2

The reason why the four New Testament Gospels are theologically similar to one another is that they—unlike most others— follow the existing gospel message of the apostles.

This second argument, then, is that the point in the first proposition is not a coincidence or a historical accident. The reason why these Gospels have a great deal in common with one another is that they come from the same theological stable. Not that Matthew, Mark, Luke, and John were written very closely together in time from a single community in one place. But they did share the same understanding of the preached gospel. For now, the emphasis will be on the first proposition, and so, to establish this, the following chapters will go through the four theological elements to see how each of our various Gospels interact with them.

CHAPTER FOUR

Jesus the Jewish Messiah

The apostolic message as Paul reports it in 1 Corinthians 15:3–5 assumes that Jesus is the Christ, the Messiah of Israel. Because this term "Messiah" was already a familiar one in first-century Judaism, the first Christians were describing Jesus in a way that other Jews would have recognized. Those brought up in the synagogue would have understood what Christians meant by claiming Jesus as the Messiah, however much some of them might have disagreed. And in fact, arguments about messiahs were not simply between "Jews" on one side and "Christians" on the other. In the beginning, all Christians were Jews anyway, and ancient Jews had other disagreements about who the Messiah was. The Babylonian Talmud, one of the central texts in Jewish tradition, imagines a debate about another potential Messiah figure, Simon bar Koziba, who led a revolution against the Romans in 132 CE:

> Bar Koziba ruled for two and a half years. He said to the rabbis, "I am the Messiah."
>
> They said to him, "Of the Messiah it is written, *He smells and judges* (Isa. 11:3–4). Let us see whether he can judge by smell." When they saw that he could not judge by smell, they put him to death. (Babylonian Talmud, Tractate Sanhedrin 93b).

First, this passage illustrates the really basic point that Jews used the term "Messiah." While the Old Testament might not be explicit about a figure called "the Messiah," the book of Daniel may have a Christ figure in mind when it looks ahead to "the anointed one (*mashiach*), the prince" (Dan 9:25–26). In any case, the term became a familiar label for an expected figure in Jewish literature like the Dead Sea Scrolls, the *Psalms of Solomon*, and early apocalypses like *1 Enoch*, *4 Ezra*, and *2 Baruch* (all second century BCE to first century CE).

The second point is that the Messiah's characteristics and role were fleshed out by passages of Scripture. In this dialogue from the Babylonian Talmud, the rabbis collectively see Isaiah 11 as supplying an essential qualification for the job of Messiah: being able to sniff out injustice. In fact, Isaiah 11 is one of the most commonly quoted in messianic passages. Also frequently used are Genesis 49, Numbers 24, 2 Samuel 7, Psalm 2, Psalm 89, and Daniel 7.[1]

Third, there are other biblical terms and phrases, not necessarily derived from particular passages, that are used to expand on who the Messiah is. The ancient rabbis, for example, commonly described the Messiah as "the Son of David," the "King Messiah," or the "Lord Messiah," focusing on his royal ancestry and status. Or titles like "the Chosen One" or "the Lord's Messiah" or "Son of God" emphasized his close relation to God. He could also be called "Messiah of Israel." These stock phrases are part of Jewish tradition about the Messiah, and we will see some of these echoed in Christian literature as well.

The aim of this chapter is to see how the various Gospels—canonical and noncanonical—use the term "Messiah"/"Christ." It will particularly explore not only the title but also the other key features of the Messiah in Jewish tradition, namely, the quotations of certain Old Testament passages and the use of stock phrases like those just mentioned. This chapter will be the first test for the theory that the canonical Gospels have key ingredients of the apostolic good news in common with each other. We will see that the New Testament Gospels contain these three features that identify Matthew, Mark, Luke, and John as recognizably "messianic" books.

1. The Canonical Gospels

The core belief in the messianic identity of Jesus is clear in the New Testament Gospels. The first half of this chapter will go through each of the canonical Gospels, looking into how they interact with the three ways, just noted, that Jewish authors often describe a messiah. We'll look in each case (a) at the basic information about where the evangelists use the title, then (b) at how they use particular Old Testament passages to emphasize aspects of Jesus's messianic identity, and finally (c) at some of the other messianic themes, idioms, and motifs they introduce.

1.1. *Mark's Gospel*

The Greek word *Christos,* which can be translated "Christ" or "Messiah," appears eight times in Mark's Gospel. These references often come at strategic moments in the narrative. Mark identifies Jesus the Messiah at the outset, starting his Gospel with the words "The beginning of the good news about Jesus the Messiah/Christ . . ." (Mark 1:1). Later, when Jesus asks his disciples who they think he is, Peter answers, "You are the Messiah" (8:29). This comes at the turning point in the middle of the Gospel. So the title appears right at the beginning and in the middle, and it also comes toward the end, during Jesus's trial in Mark 14:

> Again the high priest asked him, "Are you the Messiah, the Son of the Blessed One?"
>
> "I am," said Jesus. "And you will see the *Son of Man* sitting at the right hand of the Mighty One and *coming with the clouds of heaven.*" (vv. 61–62)

This response from Jesus illustrates the way Mark sees the Messiah in Old Testament scriptural terms. Here he uses Daniel 7, which talks of the one like a son of man "coming with the clouds of heaven," and the same passage is commonly used to talk of a coming Messiah elsewhere: Daniel 7 features in the "Aramaic Apocalypse" from the Dead Sea Scrolls (4Q246), in the apocalypses *1 Enoch* and *4 Ezra,* and in later rabbinic literature as well. Mark also employs Psalm 2 in the voice that comes from heaven at Jesus's baptism: "You are my Son" (Mark 1:11, quoting Ps 2:7). Like Daniel 7, that psalm also features in ancient Jewish messianic literature: the Rule of the Congregation from the Dead Sea Scrolls uses it, as do the apocryphal *Psalms of Solomon,* along with *4 Ezra* again. This traditional Old Testament interpretation ensures that Mark's Gospel would have been a recognizably "messianic" book.

Mark also uses familiar messianic idioms and titles, like "Son of Man," "Son of God," "King of Israel," as well as "Son of David" and "Lord." One passage in particular highlights the paradox of how Jesus is both a human Son of David and divine Lord:

> While Jesus was teaching in the temple courts, he asked, "Why do the teachers of the law say that the Messiah is the son of David? David himself, speaking by the Holy Spirit, declared:
> "'The Lord said to my Lord:
> "Sit at my right hand
> until I put your enemies
> under your feet."'
> "David himself calls him 'Lord.' How then can he be his son?"
> (Mark 12:35–37, quoting Ps 110:1)

Jesus presents his audience with a riddle here: How can the Messiah be both a descendant of David and the Lord of David at the same time? Jesus leaves the question dangling, but the Christian reader knows the answer. Jesus is human—so he can be descended from David. But he is also more than human—so he can have the title "Lord" that Psalm 110 gives him. This mysterious psalm with its two "Lord"s makes sense when we see the Father ("the Lord") addressing the Messiah, who is both Lord and the Son of David at the same time.

1.2. Matthew's Gospel

Matthew wrote after Mark and followed him closely, and so he reproduces a lot of these points. Like Mark, Matthew also identifies Jesus as Messiah in his very first verse: "This is the account of the coming of Jesus the Messiah, the son of David, the son of Abraham" (Matt 1:1). Matthew also has the dialogue with Peter and the disciples in the middle of his Gospel, where Peter declares that Jesus is the Messiah (16:16), and the title also comes up again in Jesus's trial (26:63–64).

Going beyond Mark, Matthew includes a dialogue with John the Baptist's messengers about who Jesus is. It becomes clear in this dialogue both that Jesus is the Messiah and that Jesus demonstrates the visible marks of that messiahship:

> When John, who was in prison, heard about the deeds of the Messiah, he sent his disciples to ask him, "Are you the one who is to come, or should we expect someone else?"
>
> Jesus replied, "Go back and report to John what you hear and see: The blind receive sight, the lame walk, those who have leprosy are cleansed, the deaf hear, the dead are raised, and the good news is proclaimed to the poor." (11:2–5)

These "deeds of the Messiah," then, are presented as evidence that Jesus is indeed the "coming one." The Messianic Apocalypse from the Dead Sea Scrolls contains a similar idea: "[The hea]vens and the earth will listen to his Messiah, and none in them will stray from the commandments of the holy ones . . . he who frees the prisoners, restores sight to the blind, straightens the b[ent]. And the Lord will accomplish glorious things that have never been as [He . . .]. For he will heal the wounded and revive the dead and bring good news to the poor" (4Q521, the Messianic Apocalypse).

Although there has been scholarly debate about this Dead Sea manuscript, it is likely that it contains here a catalogue of the Messiah's expected activities. The list of miracles performed by Jesus overlaps strikingly with the job description for the expected Messiah in this Dead Sea Scroll: curing the blind, healing the lame, raising the dead, preaching good news for the poor. Both Matthew and the Messianic Apocalypse make use here of Isaiah 61, which foretells the preaching of good news to the poor. In addition to other messianic passages he borrows from Mark, Matthew also incorporates Isaiah 42 and 53. These are also passages already used in Jewish expectations of the Messiah, and so Matthew would be seen as describing how Jesus fulfills that expectation.

When it comes to titles and other messianic themes, Matthew makes a lot of Jesus being both Son of God (eight times) and son of David (ten times). More unusually—but like the Messiah in *1 Enoch*—Jesus has a "throne of glory" in Matthew (19:28; 25:31).[2] His Gospel also focuses on Jesus's birth in Bethlehem, which, on the basis of Micah 5, other Jews thought would be the birthplace of the Messiah as well.[3] These and other traditional features make it clear that Matthew is seeking to present Jesus as a recognizable Jewish Messiah.

1.3. Luke's Gospel

Luke both repeats a lot of what is in Mark and has a lot of overlap with Matthew, like the dialogue with John the Baptist's messengers. Luke especially emphasizes Jesus's messianic identity in the announcement by the angel at the birth: "An angel of the Lord appeared to them, and the glory of the Lord shone around them, and they were terrified. But the angel said to them, 'Do not be afraid. I bring you good news of great joy for all the people. Today in the town of David a Savior is born for you: he is the Messiah, the Lord'" (Luke 2:9–11).

Like Mark and Matthew, the Gospel of Luke pivots on Peter's confession of Jesus's messiahship (9:20). And Luke's conclusion—in chapter 24—also refers to Jesus as Messiah in two key sections about Jesus's destiny of suffering followed by glorious resurrection (24:25–27, 45–47): calling a figure "Messiah" is often not just about who he is but what he is going to do.

In terms of his application of Old Testament messianic texts to Jesus, Luke incorporates much of what is found in Mark: he has several references to the coming of the Son of Man, evoking Daniel 7. As we have just seen, Matthew uses Isaiah 61's prophecy about the poor having good news preached to them, but Luke incorporates a large section of this chapter from Isaiah in Jesus's sermon in Nazareth when he issues the manifesto of his ministry:

> Jesus went to Nazareth, where he had been brought up, and on the Sabbath day he went into the synagogue, as was his custom. He stood up to read, and the scroll of the prophet Isaiah was handed to him. Unrolling it, he found the place where it is written:
>
> "The Spirit of the Lord is on me,
> because he has anointed me
> to proclaim good news to the poor.
> He has sent me to proclaim freedom for the prisoners
> and recovery of sight for the blind,
> to set the oppressed free,
> to proclaim the year of the Lord's favor."
>
> Then he rolled up the scroll, gave it back to the attendant and sat down. The eyes of everyone in the synagogue were fastened on him. He began by saying to them, "Today this scripture is fulfilled in your hearing." (Luke 4:16–21, quoting Isa 61:1–2)

Earlier, Luke had already called up another passage from the tradition of Jewish messianic interpretation—Psalm 89, which has had a strong influence on Mary's Magnificat (Luke 1:46–55). At the other end of the Gospel, Isaiah 53 is brought in to explain Jesus's destiny of crucifixion between two criminals: "It is written: 'And he was numbered with the transgressors'; and I tell you that this must be fulfilled in me. Yes, what is written about me is reaching its fulfillment" (Luke 22:37, citing Isa 53:12).[4]

Luke also applies a wealth of other traditional messianic labels and idioms to Jesus: he is son of David, Son of God, "savior," and "the chosen one." Luke further describes Jesus as Messiah in combinations of words familiar from Jewish tradition: "the Lord's Messiah," the "Lord Messiah," "God's Messiah," and "King Messiah."

1.4. *John's Gospel*

Despite how different John is from the other Gospels, the same pattern follows. The importance of messiahship in John is shown especially near the end. There John explains his reason for writing: "Jesus performed many other signs in the presence of his disciples, which are not recorded in this book. But these are written so you may believe that Jesus is the Messiah, the Son of God, and that by believing you may have life in his name" (John 20:30–31). The whole purpose of the Gospel, then, is to show that Jesus is the Christ, with the "Christ" title there—as elsewhere in John—explained further with "Son of God." In line with this, Martha's statement of who Jesus is provides a kind of model confession: "I believe that you are the Messiah, the Son of God, who was to come into the world" (11:27). This comes at the midpoint of the Gospel, like Peter's declaration in Matthew, Mark, and Luke. Jesus's disciples also confess him as Messiah quite early on in the story. Andrew speaks of Jesus's messiahship already in the first chapter (1:41). Jesus's dialogue with the Samaritan woman identifies him as *messias* alongside the declaration that "salvation comes from the Jews" (4:22, 25–26).

John further explains Jesus's messiahship through traditional interpretations of Old Testament passages like those in the Synoptic Gospels: Daniel 7's vision of the Son of Man and Isaiah 53's depiction of the suffering servant. He also includes other material as well. Ezekiel 34–37, for example, depicts the shepherd-prince, a new David who is going to regather the lost sheep of Israel. Jesus in John is the "one shepherd" over the "one flock" (John 10:26), themes clearly drawn from Ezekiel.

Interestingly, however, John doesn't make much of the Christ's

Davidic descent (though see 7:42). But he does include several other common messianic motifs, like Nathanael addressing Jesus as "king of Israel" (1:49). This title reappears later, shouted by the crowds on Palm Sunday (12:13). As we have seen in John's thesis statement and Martha's confession (20:30–31; 11:27), John combines "Messiah" with "Son of God" as the Synoptic Gospels do. We have seen in Matthew and Luke (Matt 11:2–5 // Luke 7:18–22) that there are certain deeds that are evidence of Jesus's messianic identity: John emphasizes this point throughout the first half of his Gospel. The miracles like the feeding the five thousand are not just marvelous wonders to relieve suffering. John calls these miracles Jesus's "signs": they are pointers to Jesus's identity as "the Messiah, the Son of God," as John 20 quoted above explains.

1.5. The Canonical Gospels: Conclusion

The canonical Gospels, then, deliberately characterize Jesus as the Messiah. In all four, we have seen, first, the fact of Jesus's messiahship. They freely use this familiar Jewish term to describe Jesus, alongside other titles. And in all these Gospels the title is given an important place. Second, these Gospel writers build on and explain the term in the traditional ways that existing Jewish literature had: the evangelists expand on *how* Jesus is Messiah with familiar messianic passages like Psalm 2, Daniel 7, and Isaiah 61. Third, the evangelists employ other familiar messianic traits, like descent from David or being Son of God. Each of the Gospel writers emphasizes Jesus's messiahship differently, but they all present him in ways that other Jews would recognize as messianic descriptions.

2. Noncanonical Gospels

Equally fascinating, and even more varied, is the treatment of the Christ title and related designations in the apocryphal Gospels.

2.1. *The Gospel of Judas*

Jesus in the *Gospel of Judas* is primarily a revealer of secret Gnostic knowledge, and is very negative about Old Testament and Jewish categories. The earthly Jesus's ministry does take place in a Jewish setting: in the run-up to Passover, with chief priests and scribes among the cast of characters. But overall, Israel's history—and indeed, the whole earthly realm—is painted very grimly. This world is made by the demonic creator god named Saklas, from the Aramaic for "fool." Probably as a result of this negativity about Judaism, the text has a very different understanding of the Christ title. It only appears once, and that is in a list of demonic rulers:

> The first is [Iao]th who is called "Christ."
> The [second] is Harmathoth. . . .
> The third is Galila.
> The fourth is Yobel.
> The fifth is Adonaios.
> These are the five who ruled over the underworld, and formerly over chaos. (*Gos. Jud.* 52:4–14)

This is obviously a fairly extreme case of how the Christ title is used. The *Gospel of Judas* does apply some other titles to Jesus. His disciples address him as "Master" and "Lord"; the people consider him to be a prophet. But only Judas knows the real identity of Jesus, as far as that is knowable. He is able to address Jesus truly: "You have come from the immortal aeon of Barbelo! But I am not worthy to utter the name of him who sent you" (35:15–21). There is some distance here from the way Jews traditionally talked about their messiahs.

2.2. *The Gospel of Thomas*

Thomas similarly has a range of titles for Jesus ("leader," "Son," "Lord"), but not "Christ." As in the *Gospel of Judas*, there is a negative attitude toward a Jewish worldview. Israel's prophets are dismissed as "dead," and circumcision is considered worthless:

> "Twenty-four prophets spoke in Israel. Did all of them speak about you?" his disciples asked.
>
> "You have neglected the living one in front of you," Jesus replied, "and spoken of the dead."
>
> "Is circumcision an advantage or not?" his disciples asked.
>
> "If it were an advantage," Jesus said, "fathers would acquire children by their mothers already circumcised. No, it is true circumcision in the Spirit which is entirely profitable."
>
> (*Gos. Thom.* 52–53)

Jewish practices like fasting, almsgiving, and even prayer are not just pointless but actually harmful: "Jesus said to them, 'If you fast, you will bring forth sin within yourselves. If you pray, you will be condemned. If you give alms, you will harm your spirits'" (14).

This negativity toward traditional Jewish ideas may well be the reason why the *Gospel of Thomas* has no consideration of Jesus's messiahship.

2.3. *The Gospel of Peter*

Similarly, another Gospel that lacks the title is the *Gospel of Peter*—at least in what survives. We have to be careful about pronouncing on what this Gospel does and does not say because we only have a fragment of it—even if it is quite a long fragment that covers the crucifixion and resurrection of Jesus. *Peter* does use various titles for Jesus, like "Son of God," "savior," and especially "Lord": "Lord" is the title that the narrator, Simon Peter, always uses. In addition to the title "Christ" being absent, Jesus is in fact never even named "Jesus" in the fragment that we have. Although the *Gospel of Peter* doesn't refer to Jesus as Christ, we do find the title "King of Israel" (3:7; 4:11), one that does often overlap with the idea of Messiah. What's interesting in the

Gospel of Peter, though, is that Jesus is never called king of Israel by positive characters. It's a label used by his opponents. So it's unclear whether the *Gospel of Peter* approves of the title or not. As we'll see later in chapter 7, the *Gospel of Peter* is negative toward Jews and Jewish institutions, as *Judas* and *Thomas* are. "King of Israel," then, may not be a title the author is happy with.

2.4. *The Gospel of Philip*

In contrast to these first three cases, the Valentinian *Gospel of Philip* does happily call Jesus "Christ." *Philip* explains this name from the second of the two initiation rituals that Valentinians used. There is the normal baptism used by other Christians, but also their own special anointing with oil, or "chrism": "Chrism is superior to baptism. We are called Christians from the word 'chrism,' not from the word 'baptism.' Christ also has his name from chrism, for the Father anointed the Son, the Son anointed the apostles, and the apostles anointed us" (*Gos. Phil.* 95).

A further significance that the *Gospel of Philip* gives to the Christ title is quite original: "The apostles who came before us called him 'Jesus, Nazoraean, Messiah,' which means 'Jesus, Nazoraean, Christ.' The last name is 'Christ,' the first is 'Jesus' and the one in the middle is 'Nazarene.' 'Messiah' has two meanings, both 'Christ' and 'measured.' 'Jesus' in Hebrew means 'redemption.' 'Nazara' means 'truth,' and so 'Nazarene' means 'truth.' The Christ is the one who is 'measured,' and so the 'Nazarene' and 'Jesus' are measured" (*Gos. Phil.* 47).

Aware of the original Hebrew form (in its Greek spelling, *messias*), the author knows that the Hebrew or Aramaic verb *mashach* (normally, "to anoint") also has another, unrelated meaning: "to measure." The author is probably implying here a theological idea found elsewhere: the Father is immeasurable, but the Son Jesus is a kind of "tailored" measuring of the Father, enabling God to be seen and understood. Despite its linguistic interest in the Hebrew, the *Gospel of Philip* doesn't explain Jesus's messiahship by giving him roles and characteristics based on Old Testament passages. The power who made the world is a weak figure who created incompetently (*Gos. Phil.* 99), implying a negative view of the Old Testament creator God. This sense of messiahship is at some distance from the traditional Jewish way of thinking.

2.5. *The Gospel of Truth*

The *Gospel of Truth* comes from the same Valentinian stable as the *Gospel of Philip,* and also has a liking for the Christ title. Here again we can see the Valentinians' interest both in names and in anointing, as in the *Gospel of Philip*. The Christ label appears at two points in the Gospel. The first doesn't attach much meaning to the term, but in the second the significance comes through. The author taps into the original sense of "Christ" as "ointment," and so Jesus the Christ is the one who *anoints* with the pity of the Father and makes troubled people complete: "The reason Christ was declared among them was so that those who were disturbed could receive a returning, and he might anoint them with the ointment. This ointment is the Father's mercy which he will bestow upon them. Those whom he has anointed are those who have become perfect" (*Gos. Truth* 36:13–20). The author goes on to talk about how human beings can be thought of as like jars. True disciples are full of oil, and then are "sealed" by an ointment—a reference to the "chrism" that we have just seen in the *Gospel of Philip*. The passage goes on, however, to warn against breaking the anointing seal, which would lead to the vessel becoming empty.

For the author of the *Gospel of Truth,* then, the Christ title is an important and theologically rich one. But it is the root meaning of the Greek word and the Valentinian initiation ritual that give it its significance, rather than the Jewish messianic tradition. In both these Valentinian Gospels, Jesus's connection with the creator God, the history of Israel, and Jewish messianic ideas is severed. In the *Gospel of Truth* and *Gospel of Philip* we don't see the authors using familiar Old Testament messianic passages to illuminate what sort of Messiah Jesus is. In both Gospels there are other ideas brought in to explain what "Christ" means.

2.6. *The Gospel of the Egyptians*

The same interest in anointing is reflected in the Coptic *Gospel of the Egyptians*, though with an even greater separation from the creator God and the Old Testament: the *Egyptian Gospel* has a parallel passage to the *Gospel of Judas*'s account of the demonic Saklas's creation of the world (*Gos. Eg.* III 57:16–19). The creator figure in Valentinian thought that we've just touched on was only incompetent; in the "Gnostic" view of the *Gospel of the Egyptians*, he's actually evil—like in the *Gospel of Judas*.

The Christ figure, though, is positive. He is called "the Great Christ," and the connection with anointing is retained: "Then the Triple-Male Child of the Great Christ, whom the [Great] Invisible Spirit—whose power was given the name Ainon—had anointed, gave praise to the Great Invisible Spirit and his female-male virgin Yoel and the silently silent silence" (*Gos. Eg.* IV 55:11–18). On the other hand, this Great Christ is split from the figure of Jesus. The Christ figure isn't second in the hierarchy of the heavenly bureaucracy after the Great Invisible Spirit, and "Jesus" is even lower down, separated from the Great Christ by two or three begettings. The savior figure in the *Egyptian Gospel* is Seth—a fusion of the Seth in Genesis with the Egyptian deity Seth or Set (who's sometimes a demon-like deity, sometimes a protective redeemer figure). Salvation in the *Gospel of the Egyptians* comes through a combination of the activity of "the Great Seth" and the "living Jesus" (III 63–64).

In fact, there is a negative disdain for Old Testament categories, as well as for the conventional ways in which Christian views are expressed in the New Testament: "Since the days of the prophets and the apostles and the preachers, the name has in no way entered human thought, nor could it, nor have human ears heard it" (III 68:5–9). Only the *Egyptian Gospel*, written by Seth himself, contains the truth.

2.7. *Marcion's Gospel*

Like the *Gospel of the Egyptians*, Marcion's Gospel does not identify Jesus with the Christ in a straightforward way. In Marcion's theology, there are two gods. There is a creator god, the god depicted throughout the Old Testament. He is at best interested only in justice and at worst violent and bloodthirsty. He has his Messiah, a figure who is still expected in the future, who will come and fight on Israel's behalf and redeem them. David, being an Old Testament figure and a servant of the creator god, is the ancestor of this creator's Messiah, and John the Baptist is a prophet sent by the creator god. When the two disciples on the Emmaus Road lament, "We had hoped that he was the one who was going to redeem Israel" (24:21), they are apparently expressing the mistaken expectation that Jesus was the creator's Messiah.[5]

On the other hand, there is another God, a stranger to this Old Testament world. He is the Father of Jesus—the Christ of this previously completely unknown God. This Jesus comes out of a clear blue sky, without having been forecast in Scripture. Marcion contrasts David, who in 2 Samuel 5 hates his blind enemies, with Jesus, who cures the blind. Unlike the creator god, Marcion's Jesus, like a modern liberal Jesus, only promises goodness and mercy, not judgment. The Old Testament illuminates Jesus's identity by showing what he is *not* like.

For Marcion, then, Jesus still bears the Christ title, although he is a Christ shorn of his Jewish messianic credentials. He is not a Messiah whose profile is assembled through various Old Testament passages and themes but is rather a completely new kind of Messiah. Put positively, he is self-interpreting and does not require the Old Testament to make himself understood.

2.8. The Noncanonical Gospels: Conclusion

We can see from this survey our first clear sign that these noncanonical Gospels are not a kind of alternative Bible that presents a unified view. They can't be lumped together as "Gnostic Gospels," as if Gnosticism were an umbrella term for anything unorthodox. Their use of the Christ title is very varied: some include it, some do not. A constant thread, however, has been the absence of using Old Testament messianic interpretation and of distinctive messianic idioms and themes. The only partial exception to this absence is Marcion, but we only find him using traditional Jewish messianic language in his description of the creator god's Messiah, not about Jesus. The *Gospel of Peter* is a possible exception, but is hard to judge.

3. Comparison and Evaluation

We can divide all these Gospels—canonical and noncanonical—into four groups, four ways of relating Jesus to messiahship.

3.1. *Rejection of Messiahship*

In this category are works where there are active repudiation of messiahship and a deliberate detachment of it from Jesus. The *Gospel of Judas* is a clear example of this, transferring the label "Christ" to a demon. Marcion's Gospel is a partial example, where Jesus is called Christ, but he is Christ in a totally different sense from how the creator god's Messiah is a Christ: Jesus's messiahship is evacuated of any of its Jewish and scriptural content.

3.2. *Neglect of Messiahship*

In these cases we can't know if there is deliberate rejection, as is the case with the first category. But there is silence about Jesus's messiahship. The *Gospel of Thomas* is a case in point, as it doesn't mention the title. The *Gospel of Peter* doesn't have it either, but it does have some characters referring to Jesus as the king of Israel—although the author himself may not be favorable to this title.

3.3. *Refashioning of Messiahship*

This group of Gospels embraces the Christ title but gives it new content. Jesus's status as Christ is divorced from Jewish messianic discussion, which is replaced with—for example—a focus on the etymology of "Christ" as meaning "anointed" or "measured." The Valentinian *Gospel of Philip* and *Gospel of Truth* undertake this kind of revision, exploring the linguistic potential of Jesus's identity as Christ and how it illuminates the ritual practice of chrism. In the *Gospel of the Egyptians*, too, the Christ figure is anointed. Marcion fits into the first category above because he rejected traditional messiahship for Jesus, but he does still retain the title, while changing its meaning.

3.4. *Embracing of Messiahship*

On this view, Jesus is regarded as the Christ, and is characterized in recognizably messianic ways: as we saw above, not just using the bare title but engaging in messianic interpretation of Old Testament passages and using traditionally messianic phrases and idioms like "King Messiah" or "Son of David." The *Gospel of Peter* might embrace such messiahship, but it is difficult to tell because we only have a fragment of the text. On the other hand, the canonical Gospels of Matthew, Mark, Luke, and John clearly appeal to the Jewish messianic tradition and embrace it.

Conclusion

So we have a spectrum of views—some Gospels deliberately rejecting messiahship, some ignoring it, some refashioning it, and some embracing it. Which of these four points on the spectrum is more likely to conform to original apostolic preaching about Jesus? It is extremely difficult to imagine that the apostles and other Christians at the beginning would contemplate the first two options—(1) rejecting or (2) ignoring Jesus's messiahship. Similarly, it would be very odd for those first Jewish believers in Jesus to use the title in a way that was unprecedented, as in the third option, where (3) Jesus's identity as Messiah is refashioned. This refashioning probably occurs in a context where "Christ" has become merely a kind of second name for Jesus.

It is much easier to believe that as far back as we can go, the apostolic preaching presented Jesus as Messiah, as captured in 1 Corinthians 15. To an extent, the apostles would have seen messiahship as shaped by the distinctive biography of Jesus. But since these apostles were Jews, they would also have understood Jesus's messiahship in traditional ways, by applying selected Old Testament passages to explain him and his actions, and by applying various messianic idioms to clarify his identity ("Son of David," "King," etc.). And that is exactly what we do find in the four canonical Gospels.

To conclude, we can return to our two arguments, or thesis statements, mentioned earlier:

PROPOSITION 1

The four New Testament Gospels share key elements of theological content that mark them out from most of the noncanonical Gospels.

PROPOSITION 2

The reason why the four New Testament Gospels are theologically similar to one another is that they—unlike most others—follow the existing gospel message of the apostles.

We can see from the evidence in this chapter that these statements are certainly true when it comes to Jesus's messiahship, his status as "the Christ."

CHAPTER FIVE

Jesus's Saving Death

Christian, Jewish, and Roman sources all portray Jesus as the founder of a group despite being executed in humiliation on a cross. The Roman historian Tacitus in the 110s CE describes how Nero shifted the blame for the great fire in Rome onto the Christians: "Nero supplied as culprits people whom the mob called 'Christians,' who were hated for their shameful deeds. He afflicted them with very special punishments. 'Christus,' the originator of this name, had been executed by the governor Pontius Pilatus while Tiberius was emperor. The despicable superstition was halted temporarily, but broke out again not only in Judaea where the evil began, but also in the city (of Rome), where everything outrageous and shameful from anywhere converges and is celebrated" (Tacitus, *Annals* 15.44). Tacitus was clearly not a fan of Christianity. A few years later, around 170 CE, the Greek satirist Lucian similarly described the Christians as a pitiful bunch: "These miserable creatures have convinced themselves, first of all, that they will be immortal and live forever. In line with this they scorn death, and many of them even willingly give themselves up. In addition, their original lawgiver convinced them that they would all be brothers of one another once they had decisively sinned by denying the Greek gods, and instead worshipped that crucified pseudo-philosopher himself and lived by his laws" (Lucian, *Passing of Peregrinus* 13).

Notably, both of these authors remark on the death of Jesus. The historian Tacitus supplies the information that this took place in the reign of Tiberius (14–37 CE) and while Pontius Pilate was prefect

(26–36 CE). Lucian, less interested in these antiquarian details, heightens the disreputable nature of the Christians by writing Jesus off as a "crucified pseudo-philosopher"; elsewhere in the same book he calls Jesus "the man crucified in Palestine because he introduced this new cult into the world" (*Passing of Peregrinus* 11).

The four New Testament Gospels and some noncanonical Gospels like the *Gospel of Peter* devote a surprising amount of attention to Jesus's death. But for most early Christian writers, the death of Jesus was not the tragic and shameful end of a great life, but an event of profound significance for the whole world. As noted in chapter 2, central to the apostolic good news was that the Messiah Jesus died a *saving* death. It was both the essential means to salvation and God's decisive act to bring that salvation about. Along with the resurrection (covered in the next chapter), the crucifixion of Jesus is the central "news" of the good news.

This chapter will follow the pattern of the previous chapter in tracing how the various ancient Gospel writers interpreted this death of Jesus in their depiction of the good news.

1. The Death of Jesus in the Canonical Gospels

The idea that Jesus's death was an atoning sacrifice or redemptive act, saving people from judgment and reconciling people to God, is prominent across the New Testament. The Gospels focus not so much on explaining the crucifixion as on describing it. At the same time, they do offer sufficient illumination for us to see some of what each evangelist understands Jesus to be accomplishing in his death. As in the previous chapter about Jesus's Jewish messiahship, this chapter also will treat each Gospel on its own terms.

1.1. Mark's Gospel

Mark is brief, but clear on the saving significance of Jesus's death. Two statements are especially important.

First, Mark taps into the so-called ransom saying of Jesus: that "the Son of Man came not to be served, but to serve, and to give his life as a ransom for many" (10:45). Here the people of God have clearly incurred a debt, and "debt" in the Bible is a common image for sin against God; often God "repays" the debt of sin by bringing punishment.[1] But miraculously, and counterintuitively, in God's dealings with his own people,

> he does not treat us as our sins deserve
> or repay us according to our iniquities. (Ps 103:10)

The explanation of how this is possible comes in Mark's ransom saying. The price on the head of God's people has been paid by Christ, the Son of Man. Ransom here in Mark 10:45 does not mean "redemption" in the general sense of salvation. Nor is there a particularly strong echo here of the "suffering servant" from Isaiah 53. Instead, the language of the ransom saying follows other ransom language in the Bible and elsewhere: the imagery is primarily financial.[2] God has taken on the ransom price for his people, and thereby rescued them from the jeopardy of judgment.

Second, Mark reports on the Last Supper, when Jesus declares that his body and blood are given for his people (14:22–25): Jesus says that his "blood" inaugurates or renews the "covenant" between God and his people, and this blood is shed "for many." The covenant point will be fleshed out further in the section on Luke below. For now, in addition to the ransom saying, Jesus's blood being shed "for many" points again to his death as the means of blessing for God's people (14:24). In this case, there probably is an echo of Isaiah's "suffering servant": just as the servant "poured out" his "life" for the sins of "many" in Isaiah 53:12, so Jesus's "blood" is "poured out" for "many" in Mark 14:24.

1.2. Matthew's Gospel

At the very beginning of his Gospel, Matthew has a unique explanation for why Jesus is called what he is. As the angel says to Joseph about

Mary: "She will give birth to a son, and you are to give him the name Jesus, because he will save his people from their sins" (Matt 1:21). Matthew has made an earth-shattering statement here. But it is also an enigmatic statement at this point in the story. How will Jesus save his people from their sins? Who are "Jesus's people"?

As Matthew's narrative unfolds, he gradually answers these questions. There are many foreshadowings of Jesus's death. The Son of Man will be delivered into the hands of men (17:22), specifically the chief priests and the scribes, and then the gentiles (20:18–19). Jesus is going to suffer (17:12) and will be "in the heart of the earth for three days and three nights" (12:40). An indirect answer to the question of how Jesus will save his people from their sins comes in Matthew's repetition of the ransom saying of Jesus, already cited by Mark: Jesus will "give his life as a ransom for many" (20:28). As already noted, this implies a price on the heads of many people.

On the eve of his death, and twenty-five chapters after the question is introduced, Matthew provides a final, clear answer to the question of how Jesus will bring salvation from sins: "While they were eating, Jesus took bread, and having said a blessing, broke it, and gave it to his disciples, saying, 'Take it and eat; this is my body.' Then he took a cup, and gave thanks, and offered it to them, saying, 'Drink from it, all of you. *This is my blood of the covenant, which is poured out for many for the forgiveness of sins*'" (26:26–28).

The mystery is solved: Jesus "will save his people from their sins" (1:21) by shedding his "blood of the covenant, which is poured out for many for the forgiveness of sins" (26:28). Jesus giving his life as a ransom, and the shedding of his blood for the forgiveness of sins, amount to the same thing: the death of Jesus brings about the salvation of Jesus's people from their sins.

And who are these people? This question also has an unfolding answer. In the course of his ministry, Jesus states clearly that he "was sent only to the lost sheep of Israel" (15:24). In line with that, when he sends the twelve disciples out on mission during his own ministry, he instructs them: "Do not go among the Gentiles or enter any town of the Samaritans. Go rather to the lost sheep of the house of Israel" (10:5–6). But with his death and resurrection, a decisive shift takes place. Even during his ministry there are occasional hints of non-Jews coming into God's kingdom. One of the preeminent examples of faith in Matthew's Gospel is a Roman centurion, prompting Jesus's prediction that, in the future, "many will come from the east and the west, and recline to eat with Abraham, Isaac and Jacob in the kingdom of heaven" (8:11). The servant Messiah will proclaim justice to the nations, and they will put their hope in him (12:18–21, citing Isa 42:1–4). These future expectations in chapters 8 and 12 find their fulfillments in the closing words of the Gospel: "Therefore go and make disciples of all nations, baptizing them in the name of the Father and of the Son and of the Holy Spirit, and teaching them to observe everything I have commanded you. And surely I am with you always, to the very end of the age" (Matt 28:19–20).

For Matthew, then, Jesus's death brings about redemption for people in every corner of the world.

1.3. *Luke's Gospel*

Luke attaches great significance to the death of Jesus. Just as John can say with Jesus's death, "it is finished," so Luke can also refer to Jesus's death as the completion of his work. Jesus says that on the day of his death "I will be finished" (13:32), and that he longs for his figurative "baptism" under the earth to be complete (12:50). On the eve of his death, he refers to this completion as imminent: "For I declare to you that what is written must find its fulfilment in me: '*And he was numbered with the transgressors.*' And indeed all this about me is coming to its completion" (22:37). Jesus here quotes from the suffering servant passage in Isaiah 53 in order to give an interpretation of his death.

Like Mark and Matthew, Luke also uses Jesus's words at the Last Supper as a key way to explain what is going on in the crucifixion. (The other principal explanation comes in Luke's sequel, in Acts 20:28.) Here Jesus declares first that his body is given "for you" (Luke 22:19).

This is followed up with a similar statement that Jesus's blood is also poured out "for you" (22:20). On their own, these statements describe Jesus's death as a means of blessing in quite a general sense.

Luke provides a more specific and profound explanation in Jesus's statement that "this cup is the new covenant in my blood." In other words, Jesus's "blood" inaugurates or renews the "covenant" between God and his people. This reference to the covenant in blood is extraordinary because it shows that Jesus's death is the entire means by which divine-human relations are restored (22:20). Some scholars think that Luke de-emphasizes the saving significance of Jesus's death because he does not include the ransom saying. But clearly Luke thinks that Jesus's death creates or restores the covenant, which is the whole framework for the relationship between God and his people. Luke, like Mark, emphasizes in this final teaching of Jesus the essential saving effects of his death.

Other elements in the passion narratives in Matthew, Mark, and Luke probably hint at the saving effects of Jesus's death. Jesus's "cup" may well be the cup of God's judgment. Likewise, the darkness that comes at noon may indicate that the crucifixion is a moment of judgment. The release of a terrorist called Barabbas rather than Jesus may imply that, just as Jesus dies where Barabbas should, so Jesus dies in the place of others too. Similarly, the curtain in the temple being torn probably implies that access to God is made wide open. These narrative examples are more controversial, because they are not directly explained by the evangelists.[3] In the light of the clear statements about the saving significance of Jesus's death, though, some of them at least probably point to aspects of this truth.

1.4. John's Gospel

Finally, John's Gospel follows a similar "unfolding" to the way Matthew's Gospel develops. In John, we have an initial statement that Jesus is "the Lamb of God, who takes away the sin of the world" (1:29). But, again as in Matthew, it is unclear exactly how this will be accomplished at that point in the Gospel narrative. As the Gospel unfolds, it becomes clear that it is Jesus's death that is going to bring salvation:

- In chapter 3, the Son of Man must be "lifted up" so that everyone who believes will receive eternal life (3:14–15).
- In chapter 6, Jesus gives his flesh and blood for the world, stating that those who eat and drink them will receive eternal life (6:33, 48–51, 53–58).
- In chapter 10, Jesus is the good shepherd who lays down his life for his flock (10:11, 15).
- In chapter 11, the high priest Caiaphas unwittingly, yet prophetically, announces that one man should die instead of the whole nation perishing. Jesus's death is therefore a substitution (11:49–52; cf. 18:14).
- In chapter 12, Jesus is the grain that dies and so produces lots of wheat (12:24).
- Also in chapter 12, Jesus foretells that when he is lifted up on the cross, he will draw all people to himself (12:32).
- In chapter 13, Jesus washes the disciples' feet, which is needed because the disciples can have no part in Jesus unless they are washed (13:8). The disciples do not understand this until later (13:7), because Jesus's service to them makes them clean, but not only in a physical sense (13:10).
- In chapter 15, Jesus calls the disciples his friends, and says: "Greater love has no man than this: to lay down his life for his friends" (15:13). John therefore refers to Jesus's death as a death in place of his friends, echoing a motif common in the ancient world.

John is even more specific about explaining Jesus's death outside the Gospel in his first epistle. Here "the blood of Jesus . . . purifies us from every sin" (1 John 1:7; cf. 1:9); Jesus is the "propitiation for our sins" (2:2) or "the atoning sacrifice for our sins" (4:10). In the epistle, then, John is teaching in explicitly doctrinal terms, whereas in his Gospel, he sets out the meaning of Jesus's death in metaphors like those of the shepherd and the kernel of wheat. But both the epistle and the Gospel are abundantly clear.

1.5. The Canonical Gospels: Conclusion

The aim in the first half of this chapter has been to illustrate both the diversity of the canonical Gospels and what they have in common. Only Mark and Matthew, for example, describe Jesus's death as a ransom; only John depicts Jesus as "the Lamb of God, who takes away the sin of the world." But behind this diversity, there is a common understanding of Jesus's death as essential for salvation. Scholars sometimes underestimate Luke's Gospel on this point, but when Jesus talks in Luke 22 of "the new covenant in my blood," it is clear that the whole framework of divine-human relations depends on Jesus's death. Although John's Gospel is so different from the others, he is in full agreement with Matthew, Mark, and Luke about the saving significance of Jesus's crucifixion. And in agreeing with one another on this point, the four evangelists also find themselves in agreement with the earliest Christian proclamation of the apostles in the message of the good news.[4]

2. The Death of Jesus in the Noncanonical Gospels

A variety of views on this point appears in our selection of apocryphal Gospels. Again, as in the case of Jesus as the "Christ," the noncanonical Gospels do not provide a unified "heretical" view of Jesus's death on the cross. On the other hand, there are similarities among some of them, especially among those that share a common Valentinian theology (*Truth, Philip*) or a Gnostic outlook (*Judas, Egyptians*).

2.1. The Gospel of Truth

Beginning with the Valentinian Gospels, we saw earlier that the *Gospel of Truth*—like the *Gospel of Philip*—was produced by disciples of the second-century intellectual Valentinus. The *Gospel of Truth* is not shy about referring to the death of Jesus and highlights two problems with humanity and the two remedies Jesus brings.

The first problem is ignorance, and so Jesus, in both his life and his death, brings illuminating knowledge: "Jesus Christ enlightened those who were in darkness through oblivion. He enlightened them; he showed a way; and the way is the truth which he taught them. For this reason, Error grew angry with him, persecuted him, was distressed at him, but was brought to nothing. He (Jesus) was nailed to a tree and became fruit of the knowledge of the Father" (*Gos. Truth* 18:16–26). When Jesus comes to bring enlightenment, "Error"—like a demonic force—attacks him and gets him crucified. But Jesus, on the cross, overcomes the powers of Error and ignorance. The cross is the tree that Jesus the fruit of knowledge hangs on.

Second, where there is what the *Gospel of Truth* calls "deficiency," Jesus comes to bring fullness or perfection. This aspect of Jesus's salvation comes about when Jesus entered "the empty spaces":

> The purpose for which Jesus appeared, clothed himself with that book and was nailed to a tree, was to publish the Father's decree on the cross.
>
> What magnificent teaching! He drags himself down to death, though clothed in eternal life! He stripped himself of his perishable rags, and clothed himself with that imperishability which no one can take from him! He journeyed into the empty spaces of fear, and he passed by those who were stripped by oblivion, since he is knowledge and perfection. (*Gos. Truth* 20:22–39)

This last reference, to "knowledge and perfection," illustrates how Jesus comes to remedy these two problems with the world: in response to human ignorance he brings knowledge, and in response to human deficiency he brings perfection.

The result of Jesus's death is summed up in what looks like the *Gospel of Truth*'s reference to the "ransom saying": "The reason the merciful and faithful Jesus was patient as he accepted his sufferings, until he took up that book, was that he knew that his death meant life for the many" (20:10–14). Like the similar saying quoted in Mark and Matthew, Jesus accepts his sufferings knowing their saving results. Although the "ransom" is not explicitly mentioned, his death does grant the many *life*. The *Gospel of Truth*, like the canonical Gospels, assigns saving significance to Jesus's death—it brings saving revelation of the truth.

2.2. *The Gospel of Philip*

Like the *Gospel of Truth*, the *Gospel of Philip* is also a rather mysterious text and often hard to understand. The purpose of Jesus's death in the *Gospel of Philip* is not to deal with sins but to regather souls. By some mysterious means, "soul stuff" has been scattered throughout the material world, a world that is not the good creation of the supreme God but an ill-conceived jumble from a second-rate deity: "The world came into being by a mistake. For its creator wanted to make it imperishable and immortal, but failed, and did not manage what he had hoped" (75:2–6). As a result, souls are trapped here, but Jesus has come to regather them:

> Christ came to ransom some, to rescue others, and to redeem still others. He ransomed strangers and made them his own. He set apart those who were his own, those whom he had laid down as deposits by his own will. It was not only when he appeared that he laid down his soul as he willed to do, but ever since the world began he has laid down his soul when he wanted. Then he came early to take it up since it had been laid down as deposits. It had fallen among thieves, and they had taken it captive. He rescued it, however, and redeemed both those who are good in this world and those who are evil. (*Gos. Phil.* 52:35–53:14)

Here again we have a ransom, but not in the sense that Matthew and Mark mean it. As *Philip* puts it here, Jesus has laid down "soul stuff" in the material realm "ever since the world began." But this current situation is not merely an ideal part of the divine purpose: the scattered souls "had fallen among thieves, and they had taken it captive." But Christ "rescued . . . and redeemed" them. After all, souls apparently become embodied when Christ implants part of his own nature in the world: "ever since the world began he has laid down his soul when he wills." So now he has come to reclaim it.

This explains why one of the other key references to Jesus's death is rather complicated: "'My God, my God, why, Lord, have you forsaken me?' He spoke these words on the cross, for he had left that place" (*Gos. Phil.* 68:26–29). Jesus is presented here as speaking the famous words "why have you forsaken me" *after* "he had left that place." In other words, Jesus in one form rose up from the cross, and in another form stayed on it. It appears that he has left his complaining body behind after taking all his soul stuff back to the heavenly realms.

Jesus's death, then, is a saving event: in the *Gospel of Philip* it is the means by which souls escape from their worthless material clothing and come back to what this Gospel calls the "bridal chamber" in the "upper realm." So the *Gospel of Philip* can legitimately be talking about "the power of the cross" (67:24).

2.3. *The Gospel of Peter*

The *Gospel of Peter*, next, has a different theology partly because it comes from a different group (not from the Valentinians). The narrative of the *Gospel of Peter* is much more straightforward than the often-bewildering metaphorical language of the previous two Gospels. As mentioned before, though, the difficulty is that we only have a fragment of *Peter*. The death of Jesus might have saving significance in this Gospel, but it is hard to tell. In what we have, Jesus mainly achieves salvation by descending to hell and preaching the good news to people there—that's one of the first mentions we have of this idea, which becomes very popular in medieval Christian theology. We will see more about this when we get to the resurrection scene in the *Gospel of Peter*.

But for the moment, there is no clear picture of a saving death in the *Gospel of Peter,* and even the character of the death is unusual: "And the Lord cried out saying, 'O my power, o power, you have left me.' And saying this he was taken up. And at the same hour the curtain of the temple in Jerusalem was torn in two" (5:19–20). The picture here may be similar to what we saw in the *Gospel of Philip.* The talk of Jesus being "taken up" here suggests not a normal death but probably the ascension of Jesus's soul. But there is no hint of this soul being a sort of collective human soul as it is in *Philip.*

2.4. *The Gospel of Thomas*

Coming on to the *Gospel of Thomas,* the death of Jesus is only mentioned once: "Jesus said, 'Whoever does not hate his father and mother will not be able to be a disciple of mine. And whoever does not hate his brothers and sisters, and take up his cross like me, will not be worthy of me'" (*Gos. Thom.* 55). The fact that Jesus says that the disciple should "take up his cross *like me*" implies a reference to Jesus's own crucifixion. So the "cross" theme is clearly important here, but its significance lies in the fact that a disciple of Jesus has to "take up his cross like me." In other words, it is the example of Jesus that is relevant: the death of Jesus itself is not a saving event in *Thomas.*

2.5. *The Gospel of Judas*

An even more radical position appears to be taken in the *Gospel of Judas,* reflected both in the beginning of the Gospel and again at the end.

At the beginning of the Gospel, we have a scene in which Jesus encounters his disciples assembled. (See the extract back in chapter 1.) Here, Jesus sees the disciples "giving thanks" over the eucharistic bread. Rather than approving of this celebration of the Lord's Supper, though, Jesus laughs at what he says is the disciples' worship of another god (33:26–34:18). The disciples then ask why he is laughing at their "thanksgiving." The Greek-Coptic term used for "giving thanks" or "thanksgiving" here is *eucharistia*, and so the point is therefore probably a polemic against the "eucharist." By the time of the composition of the *Gospel of Judas* in around 150 CE, *eucharistia* is already for some church fathers like Ignatius and Justin a conventional term referring to the commemoration of Jesus's saving death. So the *Gospel of Judas* begins with a criticism of that whole idea of the cross being redemptive.

The reason the *Gospel of Judas* is so opposed to the idea of a saving death of Jesus is that the author emphatically believes that Jesus is not really crucified at all. Jesus states that "no human mortal hand will sin against me" (56:9–10). The explanation for this lies in the real identity of who is crucified: "(Jesus says): 'Tomorrow, *the one who carries me* will be tormented. Truly I say to you (all), no human mortal hand will do me harm. Truly, I say to you, Judas . . . you will be greater than them all. For you will sacrifice *the man who carries me*" (56:6–22).

It is clear here at the beginning that there is a difference between Jesus himself and the physical body that will go through the crucifixion—which Jesus calls "*the one who bears me*." Hence no human being can do Jesus any harm. What gets sacrificed is not Jesus himself but the man who carries him around. The real, spiritual Jesus makes good his escape before the crucifixion by leaping into a cloud of light (57:24). As a result, any contact that Jesus did have with the material realm is ended before Judas hands the physical body over to the chief priests and the scribes (58:9–26). Unusually, the *Gospel of Judas* ends with this handover, the narrative stopping before there is any trial or crucifixion.

2.6. The Gospel of the Egyptians

I mentioned above that the *Gospel of Judas* shares a similar theology with the *Gospel of the Egyptians*: both are what some scholars call "classical Gnostic" texts. As in the case of *Judas*, the *Gospel of the Egyptians* also has no mention of a death. What we find there is that crucifixion has become a metaphor, and in fact it is Jesus who is doing the crucifying. Together with Seth, his saving activity is "nailing down" demonic forces:

> Jesus who was begotten by a living Word, he whom the great Seth has put on. *Through him [i.e., Jesus], he [i.e., Seth] nailed the powers of the thirteen aeons* and confirmed those who bring forth and those who take away, equipping them with the armory of knowledge of the truth in unconquerable, incorruptible power. (*Gos. Eg.* III 64:1–9)

> The second is Oroïaēl: The second light Oroïaēl, the place of the Great Seth, and of Jesus to whom life belongs, *the one who came and crucified what was in/under the Law.* (*Gos. Eg.* III 65:16–18)

This *active* crucifixion comes twice, then—first, nailing demonic powers, and second, crucifying the realm of the law. The repetition shows that this idea is a fairly established one in the author's mind as an alternative to the passive crucifixion of Jesus, which is not mentioned. Again, then, *Judas* and *Egyptians*, as Gnostic compositions, share elements in common: in this case, a lack of any sense of a death of Jesus at all.

2.7. *Marcion's Gospel*

We know from various church fathers that Marcion had a strong sense of the redemptive significance of Jesus's death. The Latin theologian Tertullian notes that in Marcion's view, the Stranger God had set his affection on "man for whose sake he was even crucified in this prison house of the creator."[5]

In particular, Marcion attached great significance to Galatians 3:13: "Christ redeemed us from the curse of the law by becoming a curse for us." Marcion saw the term "redeem" as especially important, because it appeared to support his idea that there were two gods. Through Jesus, the good, higher God was purchasing people from the lesser creator god. After all, Marcionites reasoned, why would God buy something he already possessed?[6]

As noted already, Marcion's Gospel is based on the text of Luke, with a number of important omissions. One of the key passages Marcion used to interpret Jesus's saving work was the parable of the strong man: "When a fully armed strong man guards his own house, his possessions remain safe. But when someone stronger attacks and overpowers him, he takes away the armour in which the man trusted and divides up his plunder" (Gos. Marcion 11:21–22).[7] In Marcion's understanding of this parable, the strong man is the lowly creator god guarding his house, that is, the world, and his "possessions" are presumably people or their souls. But the *stronger* man who comes and plunders the householder's possessions is the Stranger God acting in the person of Jesus.[8]

Marcion's abridged text also retains the idea of Jesus's blood being the blood of the new covenant (22:20). So Marcion probably approved of the idea that Jesus's death brought an end to the power of the lesser god and his dealings with his creatures. He would then have emphasized the word "new" in the new covenant, not because it recalls the prophet Jeremiah's prediction of a new covenant to come, but because the "Stranger God" was in Jesus's death and resurrection setting up an entirely unprecedented and unforeseen regime with "new teachings of a new Christ."[9] So in this respect like Luke, Marcion sees far-reaching saving effects in Jesus's death.

2.8. The Noncanonical Gospels: Conclusion

There is a lot of diversity among the noncanonical Gospels in their interpretation of the death of Christ: as noted earlier, these texts do not form an alternative canon with a unified, heretical view of the cross. There is a range of views about Jesus's crucifixion: these span from skepticism about whether the event took place at all to a relatively "orthodox" understanding of Jesus's death as in some way bringing about salvation.

3. Comparison and Evaluation

We are faced, then, with a variety of views of Jesus's death in our group of Gospels.

3.1. *Rejection of Jesus's Death*

First of all, there is basic rejection of the idea that Jesus died. The *Gospel of Judas* and the *Gospel of the Egyptians,* in line with their Gnostic thinking, see no real union of Jesus with the physical, material realm. As a result, there is no possibility of the death of Jesus at all, let alone one with saving significance.

3.2. *Limited Significance in Jesus's Death*

Alone in this category we have the *Gospel of Thomas,* where the death of Jesus lies in the background in one place in particular. Jesus taking up his cross is requisitioned to provide an example for true disciples to follow. *Thomas* therefore sees only limited significance to Jesus's death.

3.3. *The Significance of Jesus's Death as Unclear*

The category of *ambiguous significance* applies to the *Gospel of Peter.* There is certainly a real death: the nails are in the "hands of the Lord" (6:21). And *Peter,* as we shall see in the following chapter, certainly sees the resurrection as an occasion for salvation. In that sense, one could say that the death of Jesus is a necessary background to the saving work of the resurrection, even if the cross is not itself a redemptive event. However, as in the other chapters, we have to be careful about dismissing the *Gospel of Peter* too quickly, because its fragmentary state should make us cautious before drawing sweeping conclusions about what the whole work originally said. The same caution applies to other fragmentary Gospels, like the *Egerton Gospel* and the *Gospel of Mary*. Both have fleeting references to Jesus's death. The *Egerton Gospel* refers to Jesus's coming "hour," as does John, and the *Gospel of Mary* refers to the gentiles not sparing the Son of Man. Neither of these fragmentary works attributes significance to Jesus's death, but we do not know what the lost portions of them would have said on this matter.

3.4. *The Saving Significance of Jesus's Death*

Finally, we have the set of Gospels that understand Jesus's death as necessary and decisive for salvation. The canonical Gospels clearly fit in this category. John's Gospel differs in its emphasis from the Synoptics, and even among the Synoptics Matthew and Mark are perhaps more emphatic about the saving significance of Christ's death than Luke. As a result, there is some degree of variety across the four canonical Gospels. Nevertheless, as a minimum, there is in Matthew, Mark, Luke, and John a clear sense that the cross brings salvation.

But this is not a completely distinctive feature of the New Testament Gospels. We also find Jesus dying a real physical death with saving significance in the *Gospel of Truth* and (even if more cryptically) the *Gospel of Philip*. Marcion's Gospel shares with Luke (and the other Synoptics) a covenantal understanding of Jesus's death, and attributes a very wide importance to Jesus's death as establishing the framework for knowing the transcendent, Stranger God.

Conclusion

In conclusion, we can draw some implications for the relationship of these different Gospels to the kerygma or early Christian "good news."

The first category—of Jesus as transcending death altogether—is clearly a secondary revision of an earlier Christian understanding of the crucifixion of Jesus. The *Gospel of the Egyptians* presumes knowledge of the crucifixion of Jesus in the background when it uses the "nailing" imagery for metaphorical purposes. Similarly, by its own admission, the *Gospel of Judas* assumes the crucifixion in its double protest against the idea that Jesus is hurt by it. The text also assumes that people already hold a view of the significance of the cross when the author attacks the idea of the Eucharist.

In the second and third categories we have two very different Gospels: one that has the crucifixion rather buried in the background (*Thomas*) and another that has the death of Jesus as a prime focus (*Peter*). The *Gospel of Thomas* is fairly easy to assess: its exemplary understanding of the death of Christ is obviously one with deep roots in early Christianity: the humble submission of Jesus to suffering as a model for disciples to follow appears in all four canonical Gospels, in Paul, and elsewhere in the New Testament.[10] But to confine the death of Jesus to this merely ethical sphere as *Thomas* does is more eccentric, and that Gospel certainly differs from the earlier Christian good news in this respect. The *Gospel of Peter* is harder to assess: it may have attributed redemptive significance to Jesus's death, or it may not have.

The fourth category of books that see Jesus's death as bringing salvation is the largest. These Gospels—the canonical Gospels, the Valentinian Gospels, and Marcion's Gospel—are undoubtedly those which were closest to the earliest Christian message of the good news.

CHAPTER SIX

Jesus's Saving Resurrection

Sometimes in Christian theology the resurrection of Jesus can be seen as a poor relation to the cross, but for the early Christians the resurrection is just as important as the death of Jesus. In early Christian preaching, Jesus's rising from the dead is not just a proof that the crucifixion "worked" as a solution to sin; the resurrection itself is a saving event. For Paul, for example, Jesus was the "firstfruits" of something in which all Christians would share: those who identify with Jesus's death, in baptism, experience new life in the present and the promise of new bodily life in the future as a result of Jesus rising from the dead (1 Cor 15:20–23; Rom 6:4–5). This same double result of the resurrection—for the present and for the future—comes in 1 Peter: "Praise be to the God and Father of our Lord Jesus Christ! In his great mercy he has given us new birth into a living hope through the resurrection of Jesus Christ from the dead, and into an inheritance that can never perish, spoil or fade" (1 Pet 1:3–4).

Both new birth now and the inheritance to come are results of the resurrection. The book of Revelation also presents Jesus as "the firstborn from the dead" (Rev 1:5): like Paul's reference to the "firstfruits," the firstborn implies the first of many. Jesus's resurrection goes hand in hand with his sovereignty over life and death, as Jesus tells John: "When I [John] saw him, I fell at his feet like a dead man. But he placed his right hand on me and said, 'Do not be afraid. I am the First and the Last. I am the Living One; I was dead, and now look, I am alive for ever and ever! And I hold the keys of death and

Hades'" (Rev 1:17–18). Given the significance of the resurrection, then, it is hardly surprising that it features in a number of canonical and noncanonical Gospels.

1. The Resurrection of Jesus in the Canonical Gospels

All four of the canonical Gospels refer to the resurrection on the third day as integral to the story of Jesus.

1.1. Jesus's Resurrection in Mark's Gospel

Mark doesn't report the resurrection as extensively as the other evangelists. (This may be because the end is lost, an issue where scholars disagree.) Nevertheless, even in Mark's Gospel Jesus states that both his death and his "rising after three days" are equally inevitable and essential: "He then began to teach them that the Son of Man must suffer many things and be rejected by the elders, the chief priests and the teachers of the law, and that he must be killed and after three days rise again" (Mark 8:31; see also 9:31; 10:33–34). In line with this, the women go to Jesus's tomb to anoint him after his death but find it empty. "He has risen! He is not here" (16:6).

It is also clearly important to Mark to preserve the reference to Jesus rising "after three days," a phrase coming in all three of the prophecies just noted. This sequence is mirrored in the narration of the Gospel:

Friday:
Mark 15: death and burial of Jesus
Mark 15:42: "It was Preparation Day (that is, the day before the Sabbath)."

Saturday:
Day between the death of Jesus and his resurrection
Mark 16:1: "When the Sabbath was over . . ."

Sunday:
Mark 16: resurrection of Jesus
Mark 16:2: "Very early, on the first day of the week . . ."[1]

It might seem odd in modern Western culture to regard the third day (Sunday after the previous Friday) as "after three days," but Jewish and Roman counting was "inclusive": in other words, the first day in the sequence was included. For example, the "Ides of March" fell on March 15, but March 10 was referred to as "six days before the Ides of March." The death and resurrection being "three days" apart was a clear sign that they were two distinct events. When Jesus died, his spirit or body did not immediately go up to heaven: Jesus is not "deified" like a Roman emperor through a spiritual ascent immediately at his death.

What is "missing" in Mark is a recounting of the appearances of the risen Jesus, but these are only missing if we judge Mark by the standards of the later Gospel writers who came after him. In all these later New Testament Gospels, we have actual narratives of Jesus's resurrection appearances. But Mark does *refer* to Jesus's appearance to his disciples. Jesus had promised before his death that he would see them in Galilee (14:28), and sure enough the angel announces that at the resurrection this was about to come to fulfillment: "Tell his disciples and Peter, 'He is going ahead of you into Galilee. There you will see him, just as he told you'" (16:7).

There is also saving significance to Jesus's rising. In Mark, the resurrection brings about Jesus's reunion with the disciples, and the implication of them regrouping in Galilee is probably for the purposes of preaching the good news. This is where Jesus's preaching began, and this is where he gave the disciples their initial calling to be "fishers of men"—which they now can fulfill.

1.2. Jesus's Resurrection in Matthew's Gospel

As he does in other parts of the Gospel narrative, Matthew incorporates almost everything in Mark as well as adding more. Matthew has the predictions of the resurrection from Mark noted earlier, and incorporates an additional one:

> Some of the Pharisees and teachers of the law said to Jesus, "Teacher, we want to see a sign from you."
>
> He answered, "A wicked and adulterous generation asks for a sign! But none will be given it except the sign of the prophet Jonah. For as Jonah was three days and three nights in the belly of a huge fish, so the Son of Man will be three days and three nights in the heart of the earth." (Matt 12:38–40)

Here Matthew incorporates sayings where Jesus compares his burial with Jonah's "burial" in the whale.[2] The saying that the Son of Man, that is, Jesus, would be buried "for three days and three nights" seems even more unusual than Mark's inclusive counting. But even this superinclusive reckoning would probably not have surprised a Jewish reader. As one rabbi wrote, "A day and a night constitute a 'period,' and part of a 'period' is equivalent to the whole of it."[3] Matthew can equally refer to Jesus rising "on the third day" (e.g., 16:21; 17:23), and as in Mark, his passion narrative follows the sequence of Good Friday–Saturday–Easter Sunday. For Matthew too, as in Mark, the crucifixion and resurrection of Jesus are separate events.

As in Mark, the women come to the tomb and are told that it is empty; they are also invited to see where Jesus had been. Matthew's main expansion on Mark's narrative relevant to this chapter is in his recording of the resurrection appearances:

> So the women hurried away from the tomb, afraid yet filled with joy, and ran to tell his disciples. Suddenly Jesus met them. "Greetings," he said. They came to him, clasped his feet and worshiped him. Then Jesus said to them, "Do not be afraid. Go and tell my brothers to go to Galilee; there they will see me." (Matt 28:8–10)

> Then the eleven disciples went to Galilee, to the mountain where Jesus had told them to go. When they saw him, they worshiped him;

> but some doubted. Then Jesus came to them and said, "All authority in heaven and on earth has been given to me." (Matt 28:16–18)

Here it is striking that Jesus appears first to some of his female disciples, "the women," identified at the beginning of the chapter as Mary Magdalene and Mary the mother of James the Small and Joseph (27:56; 28:1). They clasp his feet, so he is clearly a being with a tangible body. This is despite the fact that Jesus escaped from the tomb closed with a large stone at the entrance: when the angel removes the stone, Jesus had already gone (28:2–6).

The second and final appearance of the risen Jesus in Matthew takes place in Galilee, with the eleven disciples (the Twelve minus Judas). Jesus has been the Messiah all along in Matthew's Gospel. But here at the resurrection, he enters into his messianic rule in a way that he had not before: now, Jesus says, "all authority in heaven and on earth has been given to me" (28:18). This is a fulfillment of Daniel's prophetic vision, in which he saw the Son of Man, who similarly "was given authority, glory and sovereign power" (Dan 7:14). Christ now has saving power to reign and fulfill his promise to be with the disciples forever wherever they may be (Matt 28:20).

1.3. *Jesus's Resurrection in Luke's and John's Gospels*

Luke and John continue the trend of including Jesus's predictions of his resurrection,[4] and as before, the resurrection takes place on the third day. As Matthew and Mark do, Luke and John also portray the women finding the tomb empty (Luke 24:1–3; John 20:1–2). Luke and John also give further emphasis to Jesus's appearances.

Luke's narrative in Luke 24 is unique in having a scene on the road to Emmaus, where Jesus meets two disciples who are not members of the Twelve. His real identity is not revealed to them until they reach Emmaus and break bread together. After this, Luke describes an appearance in Jerusalem to the apostles, but we discover there that Jesus had already appeared to Peter. Joanna is also listed alongside the two Marys as having seen the risen Jesus. Luke makes a point of highlighting the dramatic emotional changes that Jesus rising from the dead brings. The women are initially "frightened," and the Emmaus Road disciples "downcast," and the Twelve are aflutter with fear, disturbed, and doubtful (Luke 24:5, 17, 37). But eventually, all the disciples together—the women, the apostles, and the two from the Emmaus Road—have "great joy," worshiping Jesus and praising God (24:52–53). Hence Jesus rising from the dead is "good news," bringing transformation for those who believe in it.

John presents the longest account of the resurrection. There are three scenes: an appearance to the apostles (but without Judas or Thomas), then a meeting in which Thomas is included, and finally an appearance to the eleven disciples as well as others like the Beloved Disciple. Notably, John emphasizes that Jesus raises himself, whereas most other New Testament authors refer to God raising Jesus (John 2:19–21; 10:17–18). Like Luke, though, John has a strong emphasis on the transformation from the disciples' separation from Jesus at his death to his presence with them, their seeing him, their knowing him and the mutual love between Christ and his followers (John 14:18–21).[5] Jesus's resurrection has brought about this dramatic reversal.

Luke and John also both insist on the physicality of the resurrection. Jesus can be touched:

In Luke:

> [Jesus said,] "Look at my hands and my feet. It is me! Touch me and see; a ghost does not have flesh and bones, as you see I have." When he had said this, he showed them his hands and feet. (Luke 24:39–40)

In John:

> Jesus said to her, "Mary." She turned toward him and cried out in Aramaic, "Rabboni!" (which means "Teacher"). Jesus said, "Do not hold on to me, for I have not yet ascended to the Father." (John 20:16–17)

> Then Jesus said to Thomas, "Put your finger here; see my hands. Reach out your hand and put it into my side. Stop doubting and believe." (John 20:27)

He can also eat:

In Luke:

> While the disciples still did not believe it because of joy and amazement, he asked them, "Do you have anything here to eat?" They gave him a piece of broiled fish, and he took it and ate it in their presence. (Luke 24:41–42)

In John:

> Jesus said to them, "Come and have breakfast." None of the disciples dared ask him, "Who are you?" They knew it was the Lord. Jesus came, took the bread and gave it to them, and did the same with the fish. (John 21:12–13)

Jesus's invitation to the disciples to "come and have breakfast" implies that he is going to eat with them in John; Luke is explicit about Jesus's conspicuous consumption.

1.4. Jesus's Resurrection in the New Testament Gospels: Conclusion

The New Testament Gospel writers are not simply copying each other's resurrection accounts. Luke and Matthew overlap only partially in their narrations of Jesus's appearances, and John even more tangentially. Mark gives no accounts of resurrection appearances at all, though he does mention in passing the disciples seeing the risen Jesus.

On the other hand, there is a good deal of common ground.

First, in chronology: with various different expressions, the Gospel writers describe Jesus's resurrection as taking place on what we would call the third day.

Second, and relatedly, Jesus's death and resurrection are separate events. The life of Elijah in the Hebrew Bible comes to an end when he is whisked up into heaven in a fiery chariot (2 Kgs 2). But for all the New Testament evangelists, the separation of death and resurrection means that Jesus is not translated to heaven at his death.

Third, for Matthew, Mark, Luke, and John, there is an empty tomb. The women in Mark go into Jesus's tomb, where an angel is present instead of Jesus. The angel reports, "You are looking for Jesus the Nazarene, who was crucified. He has risen! He is not here. See the place where they laid him" (Mark 16:6). The angel states that Jesus is absent from the tomb in Matthew and Luke as well.[6] In John's Gospel similarly, Mary Magdalene, Peter, and the Beloved Disciple find the tomb empty (John 20:1–10). In these four Gospels, then, the physical body of Jesus is no longer in the tomb.

Fourth, and relatedly, Jesus rises in a physical body. This is implied but still clear in Mark. In addition to the empty tomb motif, in Mark the risen Jesus does not appear out of nowhere but can walk around. As the angel says, "He is going ahead of you into Galilee" (Mark 16:7; cf. 14:28). The reference to him journeying around implies a degree of bodily continuity between the pre- and postresurrection Jesus. The other New Testament Gospels make it explicit that Jesus can be touched.[7]

Finally, in all the canonical Gospels, Jesus's resurrection is an event of saving significance. In Mark, for example, the resurrection is the occasion of Jesus's reunion with the disciples, and the implication of them regrouping in Galilee is probably for the purposes of preaching the good news, to fulfill their initial calling to be "fishers of men." In Matthew, Jesus's rising is also when he receives his full messianic power to rule. In Luke and John, we see the transformation of the disciples as the risen Jesus brings joy and commissions them for service. The resurrection is "good news," with a variety of saving effects.

In all these cases, then, we see a close correspondence between the canonical Gospels and the apostolic message. If it is "of first importance" and a key component of the preached good news that Jesus rose again on the third day, then this is certainly echoed in the four written Gospels in the New Testament.[8]

2. The Resurrection of Jesus in the Noncanonical Gospels

When we come to the apocryphal Gospels, we find a very wide range of opinions.

2.1. *Jesus's Resurrection in Marcion's Gospel*

Marcion only quite lightly edits his base text of Luke in the resurrection narrative. As I have already noted in earlier discussions of Marcion's Gospel, there are limits to our knowledge of what he wrote. The church father Tertullian's report about Marcion's resurrection narrative is quite confusing, leading to some ambiguity about the kind of flesh in which the Marcionite Jesus is raised.[9] But it seems clear that Marcion keeps the three-day chronology, the visit of the women (and the angels) to the empty tomb on Easter morning (24:1–3), the Emmaus Road dialogue (24:13–35), and parts of the account of Jesus and the disciples in Luke 24:36–47, at which point Marcion's Gospel ends. As in Luke, the resurrection narrative contains important themes such as the vindication of Jesus and the commissioning of the apostles.

2.2. *Jesus's Resurrection in the Gospel of Peter*

The *Gospel of Peter* contains a detailed and sensational narrative of Jesus's death and resurrection. After the crucifixion, the *Gospel of Peter*'s Jesus emerges from the tomb, his head higher than the heavens, led by two angels and followed by a cross. This is a real bodily resurrection, as is clear in the subsequent visit when Mary Magdalene and her friends are told that the tomb is empty: "he is risen and gone" (13:56). In fact, given that Jesus's head is above the heavens, it's a combination of his resurrection and exaltation.

This all takes place on the third day, as is evident from the narration of events from Friday to Sabbath to Lord's Day:

Friday: Crucifixion and Burial

> "Brother Pilate," Herod responded, "even if nobody had asked for the body, we would have buried him, especially since the Sabbath is approaching." (2:5)

Saturday: Crowds Visit the Tomb

> Early the next morning, as the Sabbath dawned, a crowd came from Jerusalem and the surrounding countryside to see the sealed tomb. (9:34)

Sunday: Resurrection

> During the following night in which the Lord's Day dawned, as the soldiers were guarding two by two on duty, there was a great voice in the sky. (9:35) [The resurrection narrative follows.]

Here in *Peter*, then, we have the same calendar of Good Friday to Easter Sunday as in the New Testament.

Unlike the canonical Gospels, though, the *Gospel of Peter* actually narrates Jesus coming out of the tomb. This is what the soldiers guarding Jesus's tomb saw: "They saw coming out from the tomb three men, two supporting one, and a cross following them. And the heads of the two reached as far as heaven, but that of the one led by them surpassed the heavens. And they heard a voice from heaven saying, 'Have you preached to those who sleep?' And an answer was heard from the cross, 'Yes'" (*Gos. Pet.* 10:39–42).

This is rather unexpected for a reader who comes to the *Gospel of Peter* from the canonical Gospels. On the other hand, the *Gospel of Peter* holds on to the idea of a resurrection on the third day, even if the author develops it in an imaginative way. The resurrection also has saving significance for this Gospel. The walking, talking cross confirms that Jesus has proclaimed the good news to the spirits in the realm of the dead, a common theme in second-century Christianity.

2.3. *Jesus's Resurrection in the Gospel of Truth?*

We can proceed to look at the two Gospels that are Valentinian in their style and thought, that is, hailing from the second-century theological school of Valentinus.

The *Gospel of Truth* is certainly interested in resurrection imagery. In a statement that Jesus "put on imperishability," the author clearly draws on Paul's great statement in his resurrection discourse (esp. 1 Cor 15:53–54):

> What magnificent teaching!
> He drags himself down to death,
>   though clothed in eternal life!
> He stripped himself of his perishable rags,
>   and clothed himself with that imperishability
>   which no one can take from him!
> He journeyed into the empty spaces of fear,
>   and he passed by those who were stripped by oblivion,
>   since he is knowledge and perfection,
>   proclaiming the things which are in the heart.
>
> (*Gos. Truth* 20:27–39)

For a start, the poetic language here and elsewhere in the *Gospel of Truth* makes it difficult to define exactly what ideas the author is seeking to get across. There could be some suggestion of resurrection, but what is more likely is that the author is drawing on resurrection *imagery* rather than talking about Jesus really rising from the dead. There are no appearances mentioned, or any "third day" language. What is probably going on in this passage is that, by dying, Jesus is getting rid of his physicality, his "perishable rags." In stripping off his material body, Jesus can regain his imperishable, purely divine nature. Given what the author of the *Gospel of Truth* thinks about visible materiality, it is hard to imagine that he would envisage Jesus returning in any sense to a physical bodily existence.

2.4. *Jesus's Resurrection in the Gospel of Philip*

When we come to the *Gospel of Philip*, we again find plenty of resurrection imagery. There is language drawn from John's Gospel about Jesus laying down his soul and taking it up again (*Gos. Phil.* 53:4–14), but as we saw in the previous chapter, this has a different meaning from its usage in John. There is language about the "resurrection" of believers, in the author's description of the future state of Christians: but their resurrected forms will be made of Word and Spirit, which is a rather enigmatic description (56:26–57:8).

Finally, one passage even asserts that Jesus's rising *happens before* his death: "Those who say that the master first died and then arose are wrong, for he first arose and then died. If someone is not first resurrected, would that person not die?" (*Gos. Phil.* 56:16–20). This passage makes sense when we connect it with the passages discussed in the previous chapter about Jesus's death. According to the *Gospel of Philip*, Jesus's crucifixion is the way Jesus takes "soul"—which he has given to people—back up to the heavenly bridal chamber. When he dies, he leaves his physical body behind on the cross. This is why that body cries out, "My God, my God, why, Lord, have you forsaken me?" As the author explains: "He spoke these words on the cross, for he had left that place." The spiritual Christ "leaving that place" is how he rescues the dispersed soul stuff that had been previously taken captive: he returns it to its rightful place in the upper realm.

We can now return to our resurrection statement: "Those who say that the master first died and then arose are wrong, for he first arose and then died." This now makes sense, because the *Gospel of Philip*'s author is stating that Jesus rises from the cross as the rescuer of "soul" (*he first arose . . .*); this "rising" results in his body being left inanimate or "soul-less" on the cross (*. . . and then died*). So, as in the case of the *Gospel of Truth*, the death and resurrection of Jesus are compacted into a single event that brings salvation to the souls or spirits of the elect.

2.5. *Jesus's Resurrection and the Gospel of the Egyptians and the Gospel of Judas*

Less positive about resurrection are the classical Gnostic writings the *Gospel of the Egyptians* and the *Gospel of Judas*. They have no place for a resurrection because they do not have a real death. The *Gospel of Judas*, for example, ends abruptly with Judas's betrayal of Jesus without even reaching the crucifixion narrative:

> Some of the scribes were there, looking out so that they might arrest him (Jesus) at prayer. For they feared the people, because they all held him as a prophet. And they advanced to Judas and said to him, "Why are you here? You are the disciple of Jesus." He answered them according to their wish. Judas took some money, and he handed [him] over to them.
>
> The Gospel of Judas
>
> (*Gos. Jud.* 58:12–29)

Those words, "The Gospel of Judas," at the end are not my words but the title at the end in the manuscript: this is the conclusion to the *Gospel of Judas*. The grand finale is not resurrection but Judas selling Jesus for thirty pieces of silver, or here just "some money." It is likely that the true spiritual Jesus was transported away from earth in a cloud, in a transfiguration-like scene shortly before this betrayal scene.

Similarly, there is no place in the *Gospel of the Egyptians* for a resurrection of Jesus. As in the *Gospel of Judas,* a resurrection would be rather out of place in the *Gospel of the Egyptians.* There has been no sign of a death, and so a resurrection could not be expected. The *Gospel of the Egyptians* does contain the designation "the living Jesus," but this does not relate to resurrection but is suggestive of Jesus as eternally living and as a source of life.

2.6. *Jesus's Resurrection in the Gospel of Thomas?*

The *Gospel of Thomas* refers to Jesus at the outset as "the living Jesus" (*Gos. Thom.*, prologue). In the context of the *Gospel of Thomas,* this description probably has a similar sense that we have seen in the *Gospel of the Egyptians.* It doesn't refer to Jesus as risen from the dead as it does in Luke 24:5 and Revelation 1:18. *Thomas* does not refer to any event that might suggest resurrection, and, although there is a reference to the cross, the general thrust of the *Gospel of Thomas* points to Jesus rising above death altogether. This doesn't mean that Jesus's physical body avoids death, or that death is reversed. Instead, Jesus and his followers are unaffected by a merely material death. This is reinforced by the negative attitude toward a future resurrection of believers (51), and *Thomas*'s claim instead that Jesus's disciples will rise above any mortal limitations and not taste death (11, 18–19, 111).

3. Comparison and Evaluation

We are faced, then, with a variety of views of Jesus's resurrection in our group of Gospels.

3.1. *Rejection of Jesus's Death and Resurrection*

In *Judas* and *Egyptians* there is no real death, and so no place for a resurrection. The same is also roughly true for the *Gospel of Thomas.*

3.2. *The Collapsing Together of Jesus's Death and Resurrection*

The Valentinian Gospels—the *Gospel of Truth* and the *Gospel of Philip*—seem to share a view in which Jesus's death and resurrection are telescoped together into a single event.

3.3. *The Saving Significance of Jesus's Bodily Resurrection*

The canonical Gospels, Marcion's Gospel, and the *Gospel of Peter,* on the other hand, have a clear sense of Jesus being raised on the third day, and raised bodily because he is no longer in the tomb when disciples arrive. The resurrection also displays saving significance for these authors.

Conclusion

Jesus rising on the third day in the four New Testament Gospels, Marcion, and *Peter,* then, follows the broader early Christian message as reflected in 1 Corinthians 15:4. They all have an empty tomb, and Jesus is located elsewhere. In all the Gospels (including Mark, by implication) Jesus retains his humanity and a body. At the same time, in most of these Gospels Jesus's risen body is not subject to the physical limitations of a normal human body. Mark does not contain a resurrection narrative to indicate this clearly, but in Matthew's Gospel Jesus has already left the tomb even while the stone was blocking the exit. In the Gospels of Luke, Marcion, and John, Jesus miraculously appears out of nowhere on several occasions. In the *Gospel of Peter* his body extends high above heaven. For all these evangelists, the resurrection is "good news" in its effects as well, not just in confirming that the death of Jesus has worked to bring salvation. When Jesus appears to Peter and the other disciples, the beneficial results of Jesus's resurrection become apparent.

These depictions of the risen Jesus as both physical and transformed make good sense against the background of Jewish expectations of resurrection. For example, Josephus explains the majority view (the Pharisees' understanding) that resurrection of righteous people at the end of history will be bodily.[10] The views presented in the canonical Gospels, Marcion, and the *Gospel of Peter* make sense as reflecting the earliest understandings in the good news of the first Jewish Christians, even if the *Gospel of Peter*'s rather outlandish resurrection narrative stretches the limits.

CHAPTER SEVEN

Jesus's Fulfillment of Scripture

As we saw earlier, Paul's formula in 1 Corinthians 15 repeats the fact that "according to the Scriptures" Jesus died, and "according to the Scriptures" Jesus rose. Clearly, the work of Christ fulfilling the Old Testament—the meaning of "Scripture" or "the Scriptures" for the first Christians—was an essential ingredient in the apostolic message. This chapter will examine in general how Christ fulfills the Scriptures in his activity in the various Gospels, but with a particular focus on his death and resurrection.

1. Fulfillment of Scripture in the Canonical Gospels

It is easy to see that the canonical Gospel writers thought that Jesus's activity happened in fulfillment of Old Testament Scripture.

1.1. Mark's Gospel

The earliest Gospel, Mark, highlights fulfillment right at the beginning. After his opening statement of its subject matter in the first verse, Mark declares that John the Baptist came to prepare the way for the Lord (Jesus), in fulfillment of the prophet Isaiah (Mark 1:2–3).

The book of Daniel, especially its "one like a son of man" (Dan 7:13–14), exerts a big influence over the whole Gospel.[1] In Mark, like the other Gospels, Jesus is that one like a son of man in Daniel's vision.

Mark introduces early on the Son of Man's declaration of authority: he has "authority on earth to forgive sins" and is even "lord of the Sabbath" (Mark 2:10, 28). Those declarations of authority are followed in the middle of the Gospel narrative by predictions that the Son of Man's authority will be rejected, and he will be killed (8:31; 9:31; 10:33; 10:45). In the end, though, the Son of Man's authority will be vindicated when he returns to gather his elect and bring his judgment on the earth (13:26; 14:62).

The psalms are also crucial for Mark. Jesus is welcomed into Jerusalem on Palm Sunday as fulfilling the words, "Blessed is he who comes in the name of the Lord!" from Psalm 118 (Mark 11:9–10). This same psalm that welcomed him also contains a hint of his rejection and vindication. In the postscript to his parable of the wicked tenants, Jesus warns the priests and teachers with another quotation:

> "The stone the builders rejected
> has become the cornerstone." (Mark 12:10)

This brief sentence from Psalm 118 is important, then, because it anticipates both Jesus's death and his resurrection.

In the actual description of Jesus's death, Psalm 22 is the most influential Old Testament passage.[2] The soldiers' casting lots for Jesus's clothes is traced back to the psalm (Ps 22:18; Mark 15:24). More subtle references appear in Mark highlighting that those who mock Jesus "shook their heads" (Ps 22:7; Mark 15:29), and in the passers-by taunting Jesus, challenging him to save himself (Ps 22:8; Mark 15:29–32). Finally, there is a clear quotation of the psalm by Jesus himself, in the so-called cry of dereliction: "My God, my God, why have you forsaken me?" (Ps 22:1; Mark 15:34).[3] Mark also draws on the prophet Zechariah to illustrate the rejection of Jesus: Zechariah had announced that God will "strike the shepherd, and the sheep will be scattered," and Mark sees Jesus as that shepherd who is struck (Zech 13:7 in Mark 14:27).

When it comes to the resurrection, we have seen that Psalm 118 hints at both Jesus's rejection and his vindication. Perhaps even more important a scriptural witness to the resurrection is the beginning of Psalm 110:

> The LORD said to my Lord,
> "Sit at my right hand
> until I put your enemies
> under your feet." (110:1)

God raised Jesus from the dead and seated him at his side in heaven. So, in rising from the dead, Jesus fulfills God's command, "Sit at my right hand!"

1.2. *Matthew's Gospel*

Matthew follows Mark in many of these details, and in fact goes further into this theme of scriptural fulfillment.

Matthew's opening chapters highlight fulfillment especially strongly. Jesus is introduced as "Jesus the Messiah the son of David, the son of Abraham" (1:1). Matthew then has a genealogy tracing Jesus's ancestry back to Abraham and David. This genealogy is not quite describing a prophecy and a fulfillment, but the family tree does imply that the whole direction of Israel's history was planned by God to find its culmination in the coming of Jesus (1:2–17). Matthew's grouping of the genealogy into groups of fourteen generations probably hints at Jesus's coming as a new David: fourteen was the numerical value of David's name in Hebrew (D = 4; V = 6; D = 4, totaling 14). Matthew also adds to Mark an account of Jesus's birth and early years: chapters 1–2 identify five scriptural prophecies that Jesus fulfills, including Jesus's birth in Bethlehem, the town of David's birth.

Matthew also employs "typology," that is, understanding various Old Testament people and institutions as foreshadowing Jesus, rather than straightforwardly predicting him. Matthew sees Jesus as recapitulating the wilderness wanderings of Israel: mirroring Israel's testing in the wilderness for forty years, Jesus spends forty days in the desert resisting all the devil's temptations (4:1–11). In the following chapter,

Jesus comes to teach on a mountain (5:1–2) as a new Moses. Additionally, Matthew's presentation of Jesus as a rejected prophet follows the pattern of how Jeremiah is rejected in the Old Testament. As the genealogy sees Israel's history pointing forward to Jesus, so a whole host of other biblical figures foreshadow Jesus's ministry as well.

In terms of the passion and resurrection, Matthew repeats most of what appears in Mark. He also refers to Daniel 7 and the key Psalms 110 and 118. The predictions of Jesus dying and rising in Mark 8–10 are carried over into Matthew. One significant addition is the analogy in Matthew between Jesus and Jonah, that both are submerged for three days before being disgorged: "For as Jonah was three days and three nights in the belly of a huge fish, so the Son of Man will be three days and three nights in the heart of the earth" (Matt 12:40).

In sum, Jesus came not to abolish the Law and the Prophets but to fulfill them (5:17). This encompasses both Jesus's coming as Messiah and (included in that) his activity in dying and rising from the dead.

1.3. *Luke's Gospel*

At the beginning of his Gospel, Luke's account of Jesus's birth contains a wealth of scriptural allusions, especially in the songs. The main body of the Gospel contains a lot of what is already in Mark and Matthew. Then at the end, the resurrection narrative emphasizes that both the cross and the resurrection were in accordance with, and again *had to* take place in fulfillment of, the whole of Scripture (Luke 24:25–27, 44–46). Luke writes: "so it is written, that the Christ would suffer and rise from the dead on the third day" (24:46). Luke also stresses the fact that it's not a few individual passages of the OT that get fulfilled; Jesus fulfills the lot. When Jesus is talking to two disciples on the road to Emmaus, Luke says: "And beginning with Moses and all the Prophets, [Jesus] explained to them what was said *in all the Scriptures* about him" (24:27). And later, Jesus says to all the disciples: "This is what I told you while I was still with you: Everything must be fulfilled that is written about me in the Law of Moses, the Prophets and the Psalms" (24:44).

1.4. *John's Gospel*

John's Gospel takes it as read that the Old Testament authors were writing about Jesus. In John, Jesus says, "Moses wrote about me," and John the Gospel writer himself comments that Isaiah prophesied the way he did "because he saw Jesus' glory and spoke about him."[4] Passages from all over the Old Testament are employed to explain the saving work of Jesus, such as Jacob's ladder, which leads to heaven, the "lifting up" of the serpent in the desert (3:14) and God's provision of manna in the wilderness.[5]

As in Matthew, Mark, and Luke, particular incidents of Jesus's crucifixion are particularly said to reflect Scripture. The soldiers divide up Jesus's clothes and Jesus says he is thirsty on the cross, fulfilling Psalm 22; God preserves all of Jesus's bones, in line with Exodus; Jesus's body is "pierced" in crucifixion, in fulfillment of the prophet Zechariah.[6]

The same is true of the way John describes the resurrection of Jesus. It too is forecast in Old Testament Scripture and so was fulfilled in Jesus on the third day after his death. The evangelist comments that this was a surprise to the apostles: Peter and the Beloved Disciple, at least initially, "had not realized *from Scripture* that Jesus had to rise from the dead" (20:9).

1.5. *The Canonical Gospels: Conclusion*

It's very clear, then, that all four canonical Gospels see Jesus's death and resurrection not as coming out of a clear blue sky but rather as forecast, anticipated, in the Old Testament.[7]

2. Fulfillment of Scripture in the Apocryphal Gospels

There is a variety of attitudes to the Old Testament in our apocryphal Gospels, perhaps even within them.

2.1. *The Gospel of Thomas*

The *Gospel of Thomas* is fairly straightforward in its attitude to the Old Testament. In the middle of the Gospel, there is a dialogue between the disciples and Jesus about Scripture:

> His disciples said to him, "Twenty-four prophets spoke in Israel. And did all of them speak about you?"
>
> Jesus said to them, "You have neglected the living one in front of you, and spoken of the dead." (*Gos. Thom.* 52)

This is an interesting dialogue because the disciples at the beginning express pretty much the viewpoint we saw in the Gospels—that Jesus fulfilled an Old Testament that was about him: the twenty-four prophets stand for the twenty-four books of Jewish Scripture in one way of counting them. On the other hand, Jesus rejects this idea and totally distances himself from the Old Testament. That's the point he is making by calling the authors "dead": in the *Gospel of Thomas* that means spiritually dead. As one scholar has put it: *Thomas* "appears to sever the link with the Scriptures, contrasting the living Jesus with the twenty-four dead prophets in Israel."[8]

2.2. *Marcion's Gospel*

Marcion's understanding of Old Testament Scripture was complicated. On the one hand, Marcion did take the Old Testament to be, in an important way, true. The Old Testament was in fact central to Marcion's whole theology. It is not the case, as one author has written, that "Marcion felt that all references to the Old Testament should be erased from the New Testament. Consequently, he took the 300 major direct quotes from the Old Testament and deleted them."[9] Even for Marcion, the Old Testament is an essential backdrop to the coming of Jesus. It reports the activity of the creator God and his people Israel, and forecasts the coming of a Davidic Messiah who would come and rescue the Jews.

On the other hand, this Old Testament creator deity is not the God and Father of Jesus Christ. Christ is not an Israelite born of Mary and descended from David. In Marcion's Gospel, when the blind man hails Jesus as descended from David, other people tried to shut him up—and rightly so, Marcion thought:

> He called out, "Jesus, Son of David, have mercy on me!"
>
> Those who led the way rebuked him and told him to be quiet, but he shouted all the more, "Son of David, have mercy on me!" (Gos. Marcion 18:38–39)

Jesus has no family tree but is a redeemer who came down from heaven fully grown. As quoted in chapter 1, Marcion's Gospel begins: "In the fifteenth year of the principate of Tiberius Caesar, in the time of Pontius Pilate, Jesus came down to Capernaum." This is not "came down" in the sense of traveling downhill, but "came down" meaning he descended from heaven. At one level, then, the Old Testament, its God, its prophecies, and its Messiah have nothing to do with Jesus.

But there is also interaction between Jesus and this Old Testament deity: Jesus is the *opponent* of the creator God. In Marcion's Gospel, Jesus undoes the punishments of the creator God by healing the sick. The Gospel contains a comparison of Jesus and Elisha, which is engineered by Marcion changing the order of episodes in Luke. Marcion relocated Elisha's healing of Naaman (Luke 4:27) into the middle of the passage where Jesus heals ten lepers (between Gos. Marcion 17:12 and 17:14). As a result, Jesus's healing of multiple lepers is compared with Elisha's healing of only one. It is an essential feature of Marcion's thinking that Jesus came to rival and defeat the creator God.

Jesus therefore cannot be anything like a fulfillment of Old Testament Scripture. Marcion carefully rewrites the Gospel to ensure that there is no impression that Jesus fulfills prophecy. A lot of the passages that Marcion deleted are places where he thought Luke associated Jesus too closely with the Old Testament or scriptural fulfillment—like the birth narrative in Luke 1–2. To say that Christ is not the fulfillment of Scripture is of course to express the point negatively.

To put it positively, Marcion might have said that Christ was self-authenticating and self-interpreting.

2.3. *The Gospel of Judas*

From the beginning of the *Gospel of Judas* we see various scriptural characters and locations. The timing of the action is defined in relation to the Passover festival (33:5–6). Parts of the creation of the divine and human worlds are introduced with the formula "Let there be," and on one occasion this is answered by "and it was so," reflecting the creation account in Genesis. The divinities are sometimes given biblical or biblical-sounding names, like Adamas, Seth, and Nimrod. Adam and Eve are created with the words "Let us make man according to the likeness and according to the image." All this contributes to an impression of a concern for Scripture in the *Gospel of Judas*.

On the other hand, the creator God in the *Gospel of Judas* is not the supreme God but a minor deity, "Saklas." He only has a short shelf life, after which his power comes to an end. After the stars and Saklas have run their courses, "what has been spoken of will be fulfilled" (54:23–24). This is probably a reference to the fulfillment of some of Jesus's predictions.[10] There is no indication of any positive reference to the fulfillment of Old Testament Scripture, and it would be very surprising if there were: the creator God, the God of the Old Testament, is the inferior, evil god Saklas operating with his minions. Certainly there is no sense that Jesus's death or resurrection happens as fulfillment of prophecy.

2.4. *The Gospel of Truth*

As noted in chapter 1, the opening section of the *Gospel of Truth* provides a mythological account of the creation of the material world. The Father, the supreme God, is so far removed from everything else in the spiritual realm that he is completely unknowable. As a result of everything's ignorance of the Father, Error comes into being. Then the

Word of the Father goes forth to overcome this ignorance—an event that corresponds to the coming of Jesus to earth. So this myth comes to fulfillment in the activity of Jesus, but there is apparently no earlier Scripture that comes to fulfillment. As far as the Old Testament is concerned, there is just one fleeting reference, contrasting the tree of the cross with the tree of the knowledge of good and evil from the book of Genesis (*Gos. Truth* 18:11–33). Here the contrast involves something negative, and so it is hard to see any positive fulfillment of Genesis.

In any case, rather than there being any appeal to prophecy and fulfillment, in the *Gospel of Truth* the "backstory" to the activity of the incarnate Jesus is contained in the text itself, in the mythological backdrop. A partial analogy in this respect is John, where the Gospel's prologue (John 1:1–18) acts as a kind of backdrop to the action of the Gospel, although John makes extensive use of Old Testament Scripture as well.

2.5. *The Gospel of the Egyptians*

The *Gospel of the Egyptians* has a similar view of Israel's Scriptures. The conclusion to the book describes how it was written by Seth and also alludes to what the author thinks about the Old Testament: "This is the book which the great Seth wrote and placed in high mountains on which the sun has not risen, nor can it. And since the days of the prophets and the apostles and the preachers, the name has not at all risen upon their hearts, nor can it. And their ear has not heard it. The great Seth composed this book in writing in one hundred and thirty years" (*Gos. Eg.* III 68:1–12). So this Gospel says that no one has known the truth since the days of the prophets, apostles, and preachers, the first of these presumably referring to the Old Testament authors and their ignorance. Seth got to the truth first, and then hid it—that's why the "name" of who God really is couldn't have been known by the Old Testament authors. The revelation of Seth's words only came to light around the time that the *Gospel of the Egyptians* came to be written.

2.6. *The Gospel of Philip*

The *Gospel of Philip* displays an ambivalence toward the Old Testament. Scripture does contain "images," reflections of the truth. As we saw in chapter 1, Abraham's circumcision was an image of the destruction of the flesh, and the temple and its veil are in some sense images of the truth. However, in presenting types and images of salvation, Old Testament Scripture is doing nothing different from the rest of the cosmos: all earthly institutions, like fatherhood, marriage, kissing, sex, and even money, in various ways point to the heavenly truths in the higher realms. This is a particular feature of Valentinian theology: Old Testament Scripture is a part of a world that is not simply impenetrably evil but can be liberated from distortion and then provide some insight into the truth.

Part of this liberation from distortion is that Scripture needs to be corrected. The creation of the world was not undertaken by the supreme God but was a mistake by an inferior deity (75:2–6). Eve's extraction from Adam was as an unfortunate fall rather than part of God's creative purpose. In the Old Testament sacrificial system, Israel's offerings are not made to the supreme God but to animal-like demonic powers.

Finally, there is no sense that Scripture is a kind of privileged or inspired reflection of truth, qualitatively different from other distorted images in the world. To use the traditional terminology, if it does reveal once it has been decoded, it is a part of general revelation rather than special revelation. And the death and resurrection are not fulfillments of a prophetic Scripture for the *Gospel of Philip*.

2.7. *The Gospel of Peter*

The *Gospel of Peter* is a slightly complicated example. Here's an extract from its passion story: "It is written by them, 'The sun is not to set on one who has been put to death.' And one of them said, 'Give him gall with vinegar to drink.' And having mixed it they gave it to him to drink. And they fulfilled all things and accumulated their sins on their heads" (*Gos. Pet.* 5:15–17). So *Peter* emphasizes that those involved in the crucifixion of Jesus "fulfilled all things" (5:17), but in doing so they brought to completion their sins (5:17). The imaginary narrator of this Gospel is the apostle Peter, and according to Peter here the law is clearly demarcated as "written by/for them," that is, the Jews (5:15). Similarly, the author describes the festival of unleavened bread as "their festival" (2:5). In other words, the law seems to be about the Jews rather than about Jesus, as far as we can see from the *Gospel of Peter.* Similarly, in *Peter* it is the Jews who fulfill Scripture, rather than God or Jesus fulfilling it.

2.8. The Noncanonical Gospels: Conclusion

As in the other chapters, we see that there is a variety of impressions of Old Testament Scripture among the apocryphal Gospels. We can come now to classify these varied attitudes alongside those in the New Testament Gospels.

3. Comparison and Evaluation

These various opinions in all the Gospels on the central theme of Jesus's fulfillment of Scripture can be classified into four perspectives:

3.1. The Error of Jesus's Fulfillment of Scripture: Thomas, Marcion, Judas

First, we can see perhaps the most surprising, extreme view—that seeing Jesus in the light of Old Testament Scripture is a serious problem. This view comes out in the *Gospel of Thomas,* where Jesus rebukes the disciples for being distracted from the real Jesus by the idea that he fulfills the words of prophets who are simply "dead" (*Gos. Thom.* 52). For Marcion, too, slotting Jesus into an Old Testament framework would be a big theological mistake because it would mean making Jesus the Son of the wrong God: Old Testament prophecies of a Messiah were inspired not by the Father of Jesus but by his opponent, the creator God. The same is true for the *Gospel of Judas,* where the creator God is a negative, evil figure.

3.2. *The Irrelevance of Jesus's Fulfillment of Scripture: Truth and Egyptians*

Second, a slightly less drastic view is one where Old Testament Scripture is irrelevant to Jesus, or unnecessary for understanding him. The *Gospel of Truth,* for example, has no Old Testament quotations or references to fulfillment. Similarly, the *Gospel of the Egyptians* comments that neither the Old Testament prophets nor the New Testament apostles have understood the truth of Jesus and his relation to Seth.

3.3. *An Ambiguous Relation Between Jesus and Scripture: Philip and Peter*

Although they are rather different, the *Gospel of Philip* and the *Gospel of Peter* perhaps fit best into this sort of category. The *Gospel of Philip* does attach some value to Old Testament Scripture, because it contains hidden images of the truth just as the world in general does. It is distorted but can be decoded. Similarly, the *Gospel of Peter* refers to Scripture, but it is apparently not a text that the author himself identifies with: instead, the Old Testament belongs to the Jews, so it is their law "written by (or *for*) them" (5:15). The *Gospel of Peter*'s particular stance on Scripture seems to be shaped by the book's strongly anti-Jewish emphasis.

3.4. *The Centrality of Jesus's Fulfillment of Scripture: Matthew, Mark, Luke, John*

This final category is about the view in which Jesus's work is seen through the lens of Old Testament Scripture and in fulfillment of it—as in the canonical Gospels and possibly the *Gospel of Peter*. We don't know everything we might like to know about the concept of Scripture in these works, or even what exactly they had in their Old Testament, but clearly Matthew, Mark, Luke, and John viewed Israel's Scripture as realized in Jesus.

Conclusion

On this last run through the field of ancient Gospels, we have seen a variety of views on Old Testament Scripture and whether Jesus is presented as the fulfillment of prophecy. The New Testament Gospels fit into the final category, and so broadly reflect what we've seen in 1 Corinthians 15 as the early apostolic creed of the apostles. On the other hand, to take the Old Testament as irrelevant or even antithetical to Jesus is a position that can hardly go back to the first Christians. Even the *Gospel of Peter* and the *Gospel of Philip*, which present more ambiguous positions, fail to present the death and resurrection of Jesus as fulfillment of scriptural forecasts. Instead, their approaches to the Old Testament seem to be shaped by anti-Jewish sentiments (in the case of *Peter*) or distinctive features of Valentinian theology (in the case of *Philip*). These approaches are very different from Matthew, Mark, Luke, and John, which all present Jesus's death and resurrection as part of the divine plan foretold in the Law and the Prophets.

CHAPTER EIGHT

What's Special About the New Testament Gospels?

1. Summary: The Story So Far

In the introduction and in chapter 3, I flagged up what were going to be the two main propositions in this book. Here is the first again:

PROPOSITION 1

The four New Testament Gospels share key elements of theological content that mark them out from most of the noncanonical Gospels.

As we have seen in the past four chapters, it is Matthew, Mark, Luke, and John alone that contain all four of the key ingredients of the apostolic gospel. Paul is certainly not the inventor of this message, but he gives a very clear summary of it in 1 Corinthians 15: "For what I received I passed on to you as of first importance: that Christ died for our sins according to the Scriptures, that he was buried, that he was raised on the third day according to the Scriptures, and that he appeared to Cephas, and then to the Twelve" (15:3–5).

As noted in chapter 3, there are four key ingredients here:

- First, Jesus is identified here as the "Christ" or "Messiah." He is the one anointed by God for a particular task. "Christ" or "Messiah" is not just a title indicating a particular status. It also implied a particular role, and the role in the early Christian message is encapsulated in the second and third parts of the message.
- Second, Christ's death for sins is central to the good news. The message of Christ brings forgiveness. Present sin and divine wrath in the future are no longer a problem for those who accept the message, because on the cross *Christ* died for *our* sins.
- Third, equally important to the good news is that Jesus rose from the dead. Sometimes Christians today can emphasize the cross so much that the resurrection gets forgotten or can be regarded as just confirming that the death of Jesus "worked" as a sacrifice. But for early Christians, the resurrection of Jesus was itself a guarantee of new life in the present and hope in the future resurrection of believers as well.
- Fourth, these events were planned by God and foretold in the Old Testament Scriptures. The death of Jesus was not an unforeseen tragedy that God intervened to reverse. The Hebrew Scriptures (and their Greek translations) both indirectly foreshadowed and more directly foretold the death and resurrection of Jesus, and so the good news announces the fulfillment of those Scriptures.

As we have seen in the previous four chapters, it is Matthew, Mark, Luke, and John alone among the various Gospels that we have surveyed that contain all these essential ingredients. That is not to say that the other Gospels don't contain any of them. The *Gospel of Truth*, for example, explains the saving significance of Jesus's death, and the *Gospel of Peter* is emphatic about the historical nature of the resurrection on the third day. But none of these "apocryphal" Gospels has the *whole* good news. It is the New Testament Gospels that give the unabridged version: that Christ died for our sins according to the Scriptures, that he was buried, that he was raised on the third day according to the Scriptures.

2. Just Coincidence?

If there is a difference across all these Gospels, if the New Testament Gospels do have a different theological message from the other Gospels covered here, how did this come about? Why are they different? In the conclusion here, I want to explain the historical reasons for this difference. This brings us back to the second argument that we previewed earlier:

PROPOSITION 2

The reason why the four New Testament Gospels are theologically similar to one another is that they—unlike most others—follow the existing gospel message of the apostles.

In other words, it's not just that there is a remarkable similarity between Matthew, Mark, Luke, and John on the one hand, and the apostolic gospel captured in 1 Corinthians 15 on the other. No—they have that remarkable similarity because they're historically related: the apostolic good news influences—even determines—all of them.

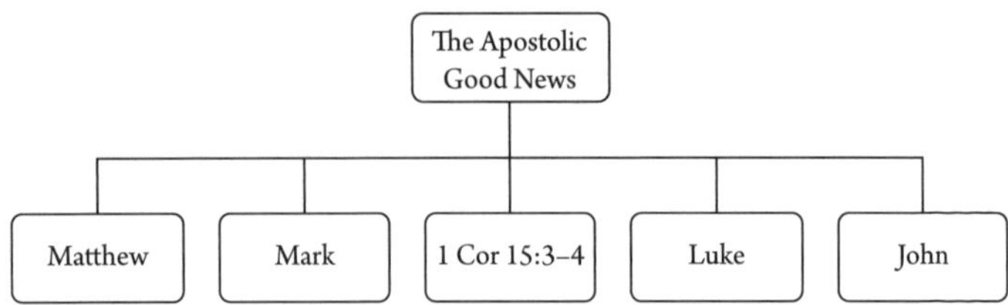

In fact, the web of historical connections is more complicated than this, because the New Testament Gospels are not all independent of each other. Almost all scholars agree, for example, that Matthew and Luke both know Mark's Gospel. But the important first point here is that all of the New Testament evangelists know the apostolic good news *because they come from churches that share that message.* We know that this message was widespread in the early church—the four ingredients, after all, reappear not just in the Gospels and Paul but also in Hebrews, 1 Peter, and Revelation, to take a few examples. And Matthew, Mark, Luke, and John are not isolated hermits writing down their own ideas in caves but active participants in the early churches: otherwise, their Gospels would never have attracted attention.

2.1. The New Testament Gospels and the Apostolic Good News

Mark the evangelist, for example, is probably the "John Mark" referred to in Acts: he has both a Hebrew name (*Yochanan* = John) and a Roman name (*Marcus* = Mark).[1] This Mark has a number of important connections. The first, according to Papias, one of the earliest Christian authors outside the New Testament, was that Mark was an associate of Peter:

> Mark became Peter's interpreter and wrote down accurately, though not in order, whatever he remembered of the things said or done by the Lord. For Mark had neither heard nor been a follower of the Lord, but later on, as I said, was Peter's follower. Peter used to give teaching as the needs arose but did not compose an arrangement of the Lord's oracles. Therefore Mark did nothing wrong in writing down in this way the various items as he remembered them. For his one aim was to leave out nothing of what he had heard and to say nothing false in them.[2]

This extract implies that Mark was very familiar with Peter's teaching, and so knew firsthand the teaching of the apostles. This is probably reflected in the fact that 1 Peter refers to Mark as—spiritually speaking—Peter's "son" (1 Pet 5:13).

The second important relationship Mark had was with Paul. In Philemon, for example, Paul refers to Mark as one of his "coworkers."[3]

Mark was apparently also related to Barnabas and went on missionary journeys with him as well. According to Acts 12, Mark's mother had a big house—big enough to be a place "where many people had gathered and were praying." So, all in all, Mark was a well-connected figure in the early church, familiar with the preaching of the likes of Peter, Barnabas, and Paul.

Matthew and Luke know Mark's Gospel, but they also have their own knowledge of the apostolic preaching. Luke, for example, emphasizes the resurrection and the fact that "The Lord has risen and has appeared to Simon" (Luke 24:34). This closely resembles what Paul says in his account of the resurrection: that Christ "was raised on the third day according to the Scriptures, and that he appeared to Cephas." (Cephas is another name for Simon Peter.) Matthew also recounts how the risen Christ appears to the female and male disciples after his death (Matt 28). The same is true of John, who probably knows the writings of his three predecessors but includes other material reflecting the apostolic preaching that certainly doesn't come from them: Jesus as the Lamb of God who takes away the sin of the world, or the good shepherd who lays down his life for the sheep, for example.[4] All these Gospel writers reflect the same good news that Paul preaches, even though these evangelists almost certainly are not influenced by Paul's letters.

2.2. *The Apocryphal Gospels and the Apostolic Good News*

By contrast, the apocryphal or noncanonical Gospels do not share the key ingredients of the good news because they come out of different religious circles from the New Testament evangelists. We have seen, for example, how some of the apocryphal Gospels not only differ from the apostolic message but actively oppose it. For example:

- In the *Gospel of Judas,* the title "Christ" is the name of a demon, and Jesus mocks the disciples "giving thanks" over the eucharistic bread: in other words, the commemoration of Jesus's death is something that is laughable to the Gospel of Judas and is worship of a different god (*Gos. Jud.* 33:26–34:18).

- The *Gospel of the Egyptians* similarly claims that neither Old Testament prophets nor New Testament apostles have caught on to the real truth about the saving message of Jesus and Seth.
- The *Gospel of Philip* appears to describe the order of events in the apostolic message as a serious theological mistake. As the author writes, "Those who say that the master first died and then arose are wrong, for he first arose and then died. If someone is not first resurrected, would that person not die?" (*Gos. Phil.* 56:16–20).
- According to the *Gospel of Thomas,* Jesus repudiates the idea that he is fulfilling Scripture. As we have seen, around the middle of the Gospel, the author describes this dialogue: "His disciples asked. 'Twenty-four prophets spoke in Israel. Did all of them speak about you?' Jesus replied, 'You have neglected the living one in front of you and spoken of the dead'" (*Gos. Thom.* 52).
- This same repudiation of Jesus's fulfillment of Scripture is an important feature of Marcion's thinking. To some degree, this key tenet of Marcion means that he removes various passages from the Gospel that imply Jesus's fulfillment of the Old Testament.

These five Gospels obviously have an awareness of the apostolic message, but they also have a clear desire to distance themselves from key elements of it.

We have also seen, though, that there are other noncanonical Gospels that don't have the same combative tone. The *Gospel of Truth,* for example, has no barbs against other religious groups, and the *Gospel of Peter* has an anti-Jewish attitude but nothing against conventional Christianity: indeed, the main emphasis of the fragment of *Peter* that we have is to show the *certainty* of the resurrection and exaltation of Jesus. But although these works are not deliberately raising controversy about the apostolic good news, there are key ingredients of that message that they neglect. So the circles in which they move obviously have different priorities about what is essential teaching. For example:

- The *Gospel of Truth* calls Jesus the "Christ" not in a traditionally Jewish sense, where the idea of the Messiah gets its meaning from a network of Old Testament passages. Instead, the author derives the meaning of the term *Christos* from its Greek etymology. And it is not just in the meaning of "Christ" that the author disregards the Old Testament: there is no sense anywhere in the *Gospel of Truth* that Jesus fulfills Scripture.
- The *Gospel of Peter* has a clear account of the fact of Jesus's death, but it is unclear what its significance is: there is no obvious sense that it brings salvation. Or again, there is no evidence in this Gospel that Jesus's death and resurrection fulfill the Old Testament Scriptures.

So, although they do not really contain much that is negative toward other versions of Christianity, the *Gospel of Truth* and the *Gospel of Peter* also appear to come from theological circles that are rather different from the source of the apostolic gospel.

All in all, then, to come back to the second proposition: "The reason why the four New Testament Gospels are theologically similar to one another is that they—unlike most others—follow the existing gospel message of the apostles." The Gospels of Matthew, Mark, Luke, and John emerge from churches where all the ingredients of the apostolic good news were valued as good and important. The other Gospels we have surveyed here may value some of those ingredients, but they also attack or neglect some of them. In doing so, they show their distance from the original apostolic good news preached by Jesus's disciples.

3. So What?

Why is this significant?

I was once asked by an anthropologist friend what the purpose of biblical studies is. It was a fair question because I had asked him what anthropology was for. My reply had three parts.

The first part is that biblical research makes a contribution to the wider scholarly field of ancient history. Biblical scholarship is at one level a subset of the whole larger study of the intersecting Greek and Roman and Jewish and Egyptian worlds that the Bible is a part of. I wrote a larger book (*The Gospel and the Gospels*), on which this shorter one is based, in order to make a contribution to that scholarly study of the ancient world in general, and early Christianity in particular. But of course, there is more to it than that. Not many ancient historians could justify their existence in public universities solely on the basis of their knowledge of one medium-sized book like the New Testament. Yet my university, which is a public institution, currently employs no fewer than four people to teach and research this book.

The second dimension of biblical studies is that it feeds into the church's understanding of the Bible. According to the Internet, estimates of the number of Christians in the world range between two billion and three billion.[5] This is a very large constituency of people who regard the Bible, in various ways, as its foundational sacred text.

Third and finally, academic biblical studies should—at least to my mind—make a contribution to wider public understanding. Despite the efforts of the four horsemen of the new atheism and others—indeed, partly as a result of them—Christianity and Jesus in particular are still a source of fascination to the general public.[6] I was amazed when I wrote an article about Jesus in the *Guardian* newspaper a few years ago and the editor told me afterward that the online article had received millions of hits and attracted a much longer reading time than the other articles in the same series (on subjects like contraception, the French election, and Donald Trump).[7] I have also lost count of the number of taxi drivers who have confidently told me their opinions of who Jesus really was and how the early church conspired to put the books of the Bible together the way it did.

It is exactly these two points—who Jesus was, and the compilation of the New Testament—that this book aims to help clarify. It doesn't try to give anything like a complete picture of either of these.

But it does highlight who the real Jesus is—the Messiah of Israel who brought about salvation for humanity through his death and resurrection, in fulfillment of Old Testament Scripture. And it also spells out how the New Testament Gospels, rather than the others which we have surveyed, are those which follow the original good news preached by Jesus's disciples. Far from being only relevant to scholars, understanding this good news is essential for all in the church—and beyond the church—today.

Notes

INTRODUCTION

1. Richard Dawkins, *The God Delusion* (London: Random House, 2006), 95.

2. In this book, "gospel" without a capital letter refers to the preached "good news"; "Gospel" with an initial capital letter is a written work, the Gospel of Mark or the Gospel of Marcion, etc. Apostles' names such as Philip refer to the person when not italicized, while *Philip*, *Judas*, etc., are sometimes used as shorthand for the Gospels attributed to them.

3. Some scholars have dated it to the fourteenth century, others the sixteenth. See, e.g., Jan Joosten, "The Gospel of Barnabas and the Diatessaron," *Harvard Theological Review* 95 (2002): 73–96 (for the fourteenth century), and A. den Hollander and U. Schmid, "The Gospel of Barnabas, the Diatessaron, and Method," *Vigiliae Christianae* 61 (2007): 1–20: "perhaps as late as the 16th or 17th century" (p. 1).

4. Ariel Sabar, *Veritas: A Harvard Professor, a Con Man, and the Gospel of Jesus's Wife* (London: Scribe, 2020).

5. Christopher Tuckett, "Forty Other Gospels," in *The Written Gospel*, ed. Markus Bockmuehl and Donald A. Hagner (Cambridge: Cambridge University Press, 2005), 238–53.

CHAPTER ONE

1. For an excellent treatment of this issue, see Mark Goodacre, *The Synoptic Problem: A Way Through the Maze* (London: T&T Clark, 2001).

2. Christopher Hitchens, *God Is Not Great: How Religion Poisons Everything* (London: Atlantic, 2008), 112–13.

3. For complete translations of these works, and fuller explanations, see Simon Gathercole, *The Apocryphal Gospels*, Penguin Classics (London: Penguin Books, 2021).

4. For this and other translations in the text, see "Original Sources in Translation" in the bibliography.

5. Clement of Alexandria, *Excerpts of Theodotus* 98.2.

6. See Mark Edwards, "Gnostics and Valentinians in the Church Fathers," *Journal of Theological Studies* 40 (1989): 26–47, and Edwards, "Neglected Texts in the Study of Gnosticism," *Journal of Theological Studies* 41 (1990): 26–50.

CHAPTER TWO

1. Herbert Lockyer, *All the Miracles of the Bible* (Grand Rapids: Zondervan, 2017), 160. See the *Infancy Gospel of Thomas* 2.

2. Quotations from Scripture in this book are translations by the author.

3. Selling possessions: Mark 10:17–22; buying swords: Luke 22:36; loving neighbors: Mark 12:31; hating parents: Matt 10:37; saving by faith: Luke 7:50; keeping commandments: Matt 19:17; perfection: Matt 5:48. For discussion of these, see, e.g., F. F. Bruce, *The Hard Sayings of Jesus* (London: Hodder & Stoughton, 1983).

4. Tertullian, *Against Marcion* 4.2.1.

5. Cyril of Jerusalem, *Catechesis* 6.31.

6. See the reference to "my son, Mark" in 1 Pet 5:13, and the "we" passages in Acts (where Paul and the author travel together) beginning in Acts 16:10. Tertullian, *Against Marcion* 4.2.1 again makes the distinction between "apostles" and "apostolics."

7. Simon Gathercole, "The Alleged Anonymity of the Canonical Gospels," *Journal of Theological Studies* 69, no. 2 (2018): 447–76.

8. Irenaeus, *Against Heresies* 3.11.9.

9. *Muratorian Fragment* 74–77.

10. Tertullian, *Against Marcion* 4.5.1.

11. So N. T. Wright, *Judas and the Gospel of Jesus: Have We Missed the Truth About Christianity?* (Grand Rapids: Baker Books, 2006), 29.

12. Irenaeus, *Against Heresies* 3.11.8.

13. Irenaeus, *Against Heresies* 3.11.9.

14. Eusebius, *Ecclesiastical History* 3.25.7.

15. See the references in Simon Gathercole, *The Gospel and the Gospels* (Grand Rapids: Eerdmans, 2022), chapter 1.

CHAPTER THREE

1. Acts 14:14; cf. Rom 16:7; Heb 3:1.

2. Richard Bauckham, *Jesus and the Eyewitnesses: The Gospels as Eyewitness Testimony*, 2nd ed. (Grand Rapids: Eerdmans, 2017), 85.

3. *The Online Liddell-Scott-Jones Greek-English Lexicon*, "χριστός," accessed January 24, 2025, at https://stephanus.tlg.uci.edu/lsj.

4. These phrases are both found in the first-century BCE *Pss. Sol.* 17.

5. Respectively, Matt 27:63–64; Mark 3:21–22; Luke 23:2, 5; John 7:12, 47.

CHAPTER FOUR

1. Gen 49:10: "The scepter will not depart from Judah, / nor the ruler's staff from between his feet, / until he to whom it belongs shall come / and the obedience of the nations shall be his." Num 24:17: "I see him, but not now; / I behold him, but not near. / A star will come out of Jacob; / a scepter will rise out of Israel. / He will crush the foreheads of Moab, / the skulls of all the people of Sheth." 2 Sam 7:13–14: "He is the one who will build a house for my Name, and I will establish the throne of his kingdom forever. I will be his father, and he will be my son." Ps 2:1–2, 7–9: "Why do the nations conspire / and the peoples plot in vain? / The kings of the earth rise up / and the rulers band together / against the LORD and against his anointed. . . . / I will proclaim the LORD's decree: / He said to me, 'You

are my son; / today I have become your father. / Ask me, / and I will make the nations your inheritance, / the ends of the earth your possession. / You will break them with a rod of iron; / you will dash them to pieces like pottery.'" Ps 89, e.g., vv. 50–51: "Remember, Lord, how your servant has been mocked, / how I bear in my heart the taunts of all the nations, / the taunts with which your enemies, LORD, have mocked, / with which they have mocked every step of your anointed one." Dan 7:13–14: "In my vision at night I looked, and there before me was one like a son of man, coming with the clouds of heaven. He approached the Ancient of Days and was led into his presence. He was given authority, glory and sovereign power; all nations and peoples of every language worshiped him. His dominion is an everlasting dominion that will not pass away, and his kingdom is one that will never be destroyed."

2. *1 En.* 45:3; 55:4; 61:8; 62:2–3, 5; 69:27–29.

3. The Aramaic translation (or "Targum") of Mic 5:2, and from the Jerusalem Talmud, Tractate Berakhot 2.4.

4. Isa 53 is used messianically in *1 Enoch*, and translated with reference to the Messiah in the Targum of Isa 53. See also Matt 8:17 and Acts 8:32–33.

5. This reference to Gos. Marcion 24:21 follows the convention that chapter and verse numbers for Marcion's Gospel follow the numbering for the Gospel of Luke.

CHAPTER FIVE

1. Debt an image for sin: see, e.g., Matt 18:21–35 // Luke 7:40–50; God repaying sin: Deut 7:10; 32:35, 41. See also 2 Sam 3:39; 1 Kgs 2:32, 44; Job 21:19; Pss 28:4; 94:23; 103:10; Prov 24:12; Isa 59:18; Jer 16:18; 25:14; etc. God also repays righteousness, or so Boaz at least expects (Ruth 2:12).

2. See, e.g., the Greek translations of Exod 21:29–30; 30:12–13; Num 3:48, 51; and Simon Gathercole, *The Gospel and the Gospels* (Grand Rapids: Eerdmans, 2022), 100–102.

3. Cup of judgment: Mark 14:36; Matt 26:39, 42; Luke 22:42; the Barabbas exchange: Mark 15:6–15; Matt 27:15–26; Luke 23:13–25; darkness at noon: Mark 15:33; Matt 27:45; Luke 23:44–45a; the tearing of the curtain:

Mark 15:38; Matt 27:51; Luke 23:45b. Matthew and Mark also have the cry of dereliction (Mark 15:34; Matt 27:46).

4. We can also note that the canonical Gospels agree with the report of the message in 1 Cor 15 on the burial of Jesus. See 1 Cor 15:4 and Mark 15:42–47; Matt 27:57–61; Luke 23:50–56; John 19:38–42.

5. Tertullian, *Against Marcion* 1.14.2.

6. For this discussion of Gal 3:13, see Epiphanius, *Panarion* 42.8.1–2 as well as the *Adamantius Dialogue* 1.27.

7. The convention in citing references to Marcion's Gospel is that the chapter and verse of Luke's Gospel are used.

8. For this discussion of Gos. Marcion 11:21–22, see Tertullian, *Against Marcion* 4.26.12 and 5.6.7, as well as the *Adamantius Dialogue* 1.4.

9. Tertullian, *Against Marcion* 4.28.8.

10. See, e.g., Mark 8:34; Phil 2:5–11; 1 Pet 2:18–25.

CHAPTER SIX

1. Since in Jewish and Christian reckoning the Sabbath (Saturday) was the seventh day, this means that Sunday, not Monday, is the first day of the week.

2. Not necessarily a whale. The Greek term means some sort of "sea monster"; the Hebrew literally means "a great fish."

3. Attributed to Rabbi Eleazar ben Azariah (first century CE), quoted in the Jerusalem Talmud (Tractate Shabbat 9.3).

4. E.g., Luke 9:22; 18:31–33; John 10:17–18; 16:16–18.

5. John 14:18–21: "I will not leave you as orphans; I will come to you. Before long, the world will not see me anymore, but you will see me. Because I live, you also will live. On that day you will realize that I am in my Father, and you are in me, and I am in you. Whoever has my commands and keeps them is the one who loves me. The one who loves me will be loved by my Father, and I too will love them and show myself to them." These themes are mirrored in the resurrection narratives: John 21:5 (cf. 14:18a); 20:19, 24, 26 (cf. 14:18b); 20:14, 20 (cf. 14:19); 21:1, 14, 15–17 (cf. 14:21).

6. Matt 28:6; Luke 24:5–7.

7. Matt 28:7, 9; Luke 24:39–40; cf. 24:41–42; John 20:16–17, 27; cf. 21:12–13.

8. The accounts of the appearances of Jesus to the disciples in the Gospels reflect the way the reference to the appearances in 1 Cor 15:3–5 confirms the resurrection.

9. On the various difficulties, see Judith M. Lieu, *Marcion and the Making of a Heretic: God and Scripture in the Second Century* (Cambridge: Cambridge University Press, 2015), 218–20.

10. See, e.g., Josephus, *Jewish War* 2.162–163; also 3.374.

CHAPTER SEVEN

1. See Morna D. Hooker, *The Son of Man in Mark* (London: SPCK, 1967).

2. See Holly J. Carey, *Jesus' Cry from the Cross: Towards a First-Century Understanding of the Intertextual Relationship Between Psalm 22 and the Narrative of Mark's Gospel* (London: Bloomsbury, 2009).

3. Clothes: Ps 22:18/Mark 15:24; shaking heads: Ps 22:7/Mark 15:29; taunting: Ps 22:8/Mark 15:29–32; cry of dereliction: Ps 22:1/Mark 15:34.

4. John 5:46 and 12:41.

5. John 1:51; 3:14; 6:32–33.

6. John 19:23–24/Ps 22:18; John 19:28/Pss 22:15; 69:21; John 19:36/Exod 12:46; John 19:37/Zech 12:10.

7. See further Douglas J. Moo, *The Old Testament in the Gospel Passion Narratives* (Sheffield: Almond, 1983), and Lidija Novakovic, *Raised from the Dead According to Scripture: The Role of the Old Testament in the Early Christian Interpretations of Jesus' Resurrection* (London: Bloomsbury, 2012).

8. Francis Watson, *Gospel Writing: A Canonical Perspective* (Grand Rapids: Eerdmans, 2013), 608.

9. Walter C. Kaiser, *The Christian and the "Old" Testament* (Eugene, OR: Wipf & Stock, 1998), 270.

10. See *Gos. Jud.* 38:12–40:26; 45:12–46:2; 46:18–47:1; 54:24–55:1.

CHAPTER EIGHT

1. In Acts 12 and 15 he is referred to as "John, also called Mark."

2. Papias, cited in Eusebius, *Ecclesiastical History* 3.39.15.

3. Phlm 24: see also Col 4:10; 2 Tim 4:11.

4. See Eve-Marie Becker, Helen Bond, and Catrin Williams, eds., *John's Transformation of Mark* (London: Bloomsbury, 2021).

5. A Google search, "How many Christians are there in the world?" on August 12, 2024, gave figures of 2.4 billion, 2.18 billion, 2.38 billion, 2.2 billion, and 2.6 billion, from the first websites found.

6. See Christopher Hitchens, Richard Dawkins, Sam Harris, and Daniel Dennett, *The Four Horsemen: The Conversation That Sparked an Atheist Revolution* (New York: Random House, 2019).

7. Simon Gathercole, "What Is the Historical Evidence That Jesus Christ Lived and Died?," *Guardian*, April 14, 2017, https://www.theguardian.com/world/2017/apr/14/what-is-the-historical-evidence-that-jesus-christ-lived-and-died.

Bibliography

Original Sources in Translation

Classical Sources

Costa, C. D. N., trans. *Lucian: Selected Dialogues*. Oxford World's Classics. Oxford: Oxford University Press, 2009.

Grant, Michael, trans. *The Annals of Imperial Rome*. Penguin Classics. London: Penguin Books, 2003.

Jewish Sources

Cathcart, Kevin J., and Robert P. Gordon, trans. *The Targum of the Minor Prophets*. Aramaic Bible, vol. 14. Edinburgh: T&T Clark, 1989.

Chilton, Bruce D., trans. *The Targum Isaiah*. Aramaic Bible, vol. 11. Edinburgh: T&T Clark, 1987.

Epstein, Isidore, ed. *The Babylonian Talmud: Translated into English with Notes, Glossary, and Indices*. London: Soncino, 1984.

Guggenheimer, Heinrich W., trans. *The Jerusalem Talmud*. Berlin: de Gruyter, 2000–2011.

Henze, Matthias, and Michael E. Stone, trans. *4 Ezra and 2 Baruch: Translations, Introductions, and Notes*. Minneapolis: Fortress, 2013.

Lee, Timothy A. *The Psalms of Solomon: Facing Greek-English Text*. Cambridge: TLee, 2024.

Nickelsburg, George W. E. *1 Enoch: A New Translation*. Minneapolis: Fortress, 2005.

Thackeray, H. St. J., et al. *The Jewish War*. Loeb Classical Library. Repr., London: Heinemann, 1997.

Vermes, Geza. *The Complete Dead Sea Scrolls in English*. Penguin Classics. London: Penguin Books, 2004.

Apocryphal Gospels and Related Sources

Casey, R. P. *The Excerpta ex Theodoto of Clement of Alexandria*. London: Christophers, 1934.

Evans, Ernest. *Adversus Marcionem: Books 1–5*. 2 vols. Oxford: Clarendon, 1972.

Gathercole, Simon. *The Apocryphal Gospels*. Penguin Classics. London: Penguin Books, 2021.

Pretty, Robert A., trans. *Adamantius: Dialogue on the True Faith in God*. Leuven: Peeters, 1997.

Church Fathers

Evans, Ernest. *Adversus Marcionem: Books 1–5*. 2 vols. Oxford: Clarendon, 1972.

Gifford, Edwin Hamilton. *Cyril of Jerusalem: Catechetical Lectures*. Nicene and Post-Nicene Fathers, 2nd ser., vol. 7. Buffalo, NY: Christian Literature Publishing Co., 1894.

Lake, Kirsopp. *Ecclesiastical History, Volume I: Books 1–5*. Loeb Classical Library. London: Heinemann, 1926.

Metzger, Bruce M. "The Muratorian Canon." Pp. 304–7 in *The Canon of the New Testament: Its Origin, Development, and Significance*. Oxford: Clarendon, 1987.

Unger, Dominic, trans. *St. Irenaeus of Lyons: Against the Heresies (Book 3)*. Ancient Christian Writers 64. New York: Paulist, 2012.

Williams, Frank, trans. *The Panarion of Epiphanius of Salamis*. 2 vols. Leiden: Brill, 2009.

Scholarly References

Bauckham, Richard. *Jesus and the Eyewitnesses: The Gospels as Eyewitness Testimony*. 2nd ed. Grand Rapids: Eerdmans, 2017.

Becker, Eve-Marie, Helen Bond, and Catrin Williams, eds. *John's Transformation of Mark*. London: Bloomsbury, 2021.

Bruce, F. F. *The Hard Sayings of Jesus*. London: Hodder & Stoughton, 1983.

Carey, Holly J. *Jesus' Cry from the Cross: Towards a First-Century Understanding of the Intertextual Relationship Between Psalm 22 and the Narrative of Mark's Gospel*. London: Bloomsbury, 2009.

Dawkins, Richard. *The God Delusion*. London: Random House, 2006.

Edwards, Mark. "Gnostics and Valentinians in the Church Fathers." *Journal of Theological Studies* 40 (1989): 26–47.

———. "Neglected Texts in the Study of Gnosticism." *Journal of Theological Studies* 41 (1990): 26–50.

Gathercole, Simon. "The Alleged Anonymity of the Canonical Gospels." *Journal of Theological Studies* 69, no. 2 (2018): 447–76.

———. *The Apocryphal Gospels*. Penguin Classics. London: Penguin, 2021.

———. *The Gospel and the Gospels*. Grand Rapids: Eerdmans, 2022.

———. "What Is the Historical Evidence That Jesus Christ Lived and Died?" *Guardian*, April 14, 2017. https://www.theguardian.com/world/2017/apr/14/what-is-the-historical-evidence-that-jesus-christ-lived-and-died.

Goodacre, Mark. *The Synoptic Problem: A Way Through the Maze*. London: T&T Clark, 2001.

Hitchens, Christopher. *God Is Not Great: How Religion Poisons Everything*. London: Atlantic, 2008.

Hitchens, Christopher, Richard Dawkins, Sam Harris, and Daniel Dennett. *The Four Horsemen: The Conversation That Sparked an Atheist Revolution*. New York: Random House, 2019.

Hollander, A. den, and U. Schmid. "The Gospel of Barnabas, the Diatessaron, and Method." *Vigiliae Christianae* 61 (2007): 1–20.

Hooker, Morna D. *The Son of Man in Mark*. London: SPCK, 1967.

Joosten, Jan. "The Gospel of Barnabas and the Diatessaron." *Harvard Theological Review* 95 (2002): 73–96.

Kaiser, Walter C. *The Christian and the "Old" Testament*. Eugene, OR: Wipf & Stock, 1998.

Lieu, Judith M. *Marcion and the Making of a Heretic: God and Scripture in the Second Century*. Cambridge: Cambridge University Press, 2015.

Lockyer, Herbert. *All the Miracles of the Bible*. Grand Rapids: Zondervan, 2017.

Moo, Douglas J. *The Old Testament in the Gospel Passion Narratives*. Sheffield: Almond, 1983.

Novakovic, Lidija. *Raised from the Dead According to Scripture: The Role of the Old Testament in the Early Christian Interpretations of Jesus' Resurrection*. London: Bloomsbury, 2012.

Sabar, Ariel. *Veritas: A Harvard Professor, a Con Man, and the Gospel of Jesus's Wife*. London: Scribe, 2020.

Tuckett, Christopher. "Forty Other Gospels." Pp. 238–53 in *The Written Gospel*, edited by Markus Bockmuehl and Donald A. Hagner. Cambridge: Cambridge University Press, 2005.

Watson, Francis. *Gospel Writing: A Canonical Perspective*. Grand Rapids: Eerdmans, 2013.

Wright, N. T. *Judas and the Gospel of Jesus: Have We Missed the Truth About Christianity?* Grand Rapids: Baker Books, 2006.

Index of Subjects

Index of Scripture and Other Ancient Sources